GOD CHOSE AN ARTIST

Bezalel's Call

Cover art and design: Alma Villegas

Inside book layout: Alma Villegas

Photo of Alma Villegas on back cover: Zahira Villegas-González

Translation by: Betty Austin Muñoz,
Zahira Villegas-González and Alma Villegas

The Gift of Art
New York & Puerto Rico, 2020

GOD CHOSE AN ARTIST

Bezalel's Call

Alma Villegas, PhD

Based on
Bezalel, an Artist Called by God

Towards a Theology of Art
The Bezalel Series, Volume 1A

THE GIFT OF ART
Connecting Heaven and Earth Through the Arts

for glory and for beauty
Exodus 28:2

New York & Puerto Rico, 2020

DEDICATION

To

Moisés Villegas Fernandez, Jr.

My beloved brother, who,
every time I have confronted a
mountain that seems to scream at me,
"Alma, this is as far as you go,"
has been by my side, telling me,
"Go forward. With Christ, you can do it."

To

Daniel Montañez

I saw how he created and directed
the first theatrical performances in the
church and created and directed the
Grupo de AVIVAMIENTO.

To

Grupo de AVIVAMIENTO

Especially to the members during the
first thirteen years of the group (1967–1980),
with whom I grew up physically and spiritually
and with whom I shared my first artistic dreams
of moving on to change the world.

Also, to all the members who have followed.

NOTE TO THE READER

To reach more readers with the message of the Theology of Art and to please those who want to read small books, we have divided *Bezalel, an Artist Called by God* in three parts. They are divided considering the main themes of the book. The Introduction, Conclusion and Appendices remain the same across the three books. They are:

- GOD CHOSE AN ARTIST
  Bezalel's Call, Volume 1A
- AN ARTIST?
  God Has Six Gifts for You, Volume 1B
- OBEDIENCE AND SUBMISSION
  The Key to Bezalel's Success, Volume 1C

SEE, I HAVE CALLED

Now the Lord spoke to Moses, saying:

See, I have called by name Bezalel the son of Uri, the son of Hur, of the tribe of Judah. I have filled him with the Spirit of God in wisdom, in understanding, in knowledge, and in all manner of craftsmanship to devise artistic works for work with gold, with silver, and with bronze, and in the cutting of stones for settings, and in carving of wood, to work in all manner of craftsmanship.

Exodus 31:1–5

Moses said to the children of Israel:

See, the Lord has called by name Bezalel the son of Uri, the son of Hur, of the tribe of Judah. And He has filled him with the Spirit of God, in wisdom, in understanding, and in knowledge, and in all manner of craftsmanship, to design artistic works, to work in gold, in silver, and in bronze, and in the cutting of stones for settings and in the carving of wood in order to make every manner of artistic work.

He also has put in his heart to teach, both he and Oholiab, the son of Ahisamak, of the tribe of Dan. He has filled them with skill to do all manner of work as craftsmen; as designers; as embroiderers in blue, in purple, in scarlet, and in fine linen; and as weavers: as craftsmen of every work and artistic designers.

Exodus 35:30–35

CONTENTS

INTRODUCTION
LORD, MAKE ME A WOMAN OF IDEAS

IN SEARCH OF A DREAM

In June of 1980, I left Puerto Rico for England and New York in pursuit of a beautiful dream: to do graduate studies in theater, with the purpose of using it as a transforming agent and so that people could see through it the reflection of a Creator God. There was in me an immense thirst for artistic knowledge that could enable me to accomplish my goals. I'd already had the experience of working with a group of young people and seeing what God could do when we put our talents and skills in their hands. However, reaching that moment of decision in my life was not an easy path. First, discovering and accepting my artistic talents meant going against what, at that time, was accepted by the Church in general, and second, daring to take the step and start moving in a way that I suspected was the will of God required all my faith and courage. Many times, people said to me:

--- "Christ is coming, and you are going to study...WHAT? THEATER?"

--- "Oh...so you want to be an 'actress'?"

--- "Are you telling me that God had called you to serve Him through the arts? Are you sure?"
--- "Are you telling me that art is a gift from God?"

--- "The Lord told me that you can't rehearse the play in the church."

These questions and statements came from pastors, presidents of evangelical denominations, Christian leaders, and so forth. I was so intimidated. And with each pronouncement, my insecurities grew. I had many questions and fears: "Am I doing something against the will of God?" "Am I doing something dishonest?" "Am I going to lose my salvation? "Am I going to hell?" "Am I becoming mundane?" I was so confused.

MY BEGINNINGS

I accepted Jesus as my Savior at 16 and started attending youth meetings. But one night, as I arrived at a youth meeting, I found out that we would have a planning session to come up with ideas and activities for the upcoming Youth Week, and I found myself unable to present any ideas. I was making such a big effort to comply with what I understood, at that time, was to serve God that I had put Him in a religious box, and as a consequence, creative ideas were not flowing because I was afraid of them. That night, I prayed to God. Right where I was sitting, I turned my face to the white wall I was leaning against, and I just told Him, "Lord, make me a woman of ideas." I was surprised to hear myself saying such a prayer, so much so that I still remember not only the moment, but the exact words pronounced. I understood that it was an inward cry coming from the bottom of my being, although I could not understand how or why those words had come from my mouth.

Until that moment, I had never had a goal for my life. I knew that I wanted to study because my parents continually repeated the importance of an education, but study what? I was only excited about music, dance, painting, and poetry, but that was something that was very far from my reality, so I discarded them from my life. Therefore, I had not stopped to think about what I was going to study, and I do not remember other dreams or future ambitions. Additionally, I discovered that if I wanted to consecrate my life to the Lord Jesus, I could not participate in anything artistic. For example, cinema, theater, and dance or acting classes, among other artistic endeavors, were not accepted in the Church. I understood that my love for Jesus was greater than my love for the arts, so it was no problem becoming a science teacher.

I now recognize that one of the first things that Jesus did after saving my life was awaken my dreams. Those dreams had been forgotten, and I had no idea they were still inside of me. Those dreams were not dead, but dormant, asleep. Before the presence of the Creator God, my dreams were awakened. And the Spirit of God, who searches everything, even the most intimate parts of our heart, made me exclaim, "Lord, make me a woman of ideas." I understand that God heard that prayer. I believe it was a prayer that came out of the heart of God, and it became a seed inside my spirit. There are moments when we believe that we are the ones praying, but then we realize that it is the Spirit of God placing the prayer into our spirit. The Spirit of God was moving over my spirit to incubate, to nurture, the calling that God put in me before the foundation of the world.

To my surprise, the answer to this prayer manifested itself through art, especially theater. Artistic ideas emerged again. I created several theater groups, wrote some plays and after several theater production, I decided to study theater, dance and visual arts. But I became even more confused. Where do ideas come from? I was seeking the Lord with all my heart, so why did I have this strong inclination towards the arts, towards the theater. The fear of turning away from God arose once again. But this time, I asked God. Only He could have the correct answer.

MY ENCOUNTER WITH BEZALEL

This was an experience that impacted my life drastically. When I felt the direct opposition that most of the churches were displaying in relation to art, a question arose from within me: "What does the Bible say about art?" I had learned that the Bible is above any revelation or prophetic word. So, with great naïveté on my part, I asked God where, in the Bible, the passages concerning art were. And I say naïveté because it seems strange to me now that

3

it never occurred to me to consult a concordance, Bible dictionary, or encyclopedia, much less ask the pastor. I thought mine was a question that only God could answer, and for the next three months, I sat in a pew in the prayer room in my church with the Bible on my lap, repeating the same prayer over and over, "Lord, show me where in your Word does it say that art comes from you."

What I discovered in the Bible changed my relationship with God and my destiny forever. One evening, my Bible fell to the floor, and when I picked it up, my eyes looked at Exodus 31:3: "And I have filled him with the spirit of God, in wisdom, and in understanding, and in knowledge, and in all manner of workmanship." But in the Spanish version, instead of workmanship, it says, "ART." WOW and WOW. The answer that I was looking for was in front of my eyes. The arts may be forbidden in many churches, but not in God's WORD. What an amazing revelation! What an amazing God!

A year after that experience, I found myself on an airplane on my way to England to study theater. And to clarify, no, my destiny didn't change; the Bible just pointed to my real destiny, and I became the theater director, playwright, and theology of art scholar that God ordained and sanctified me to be even before He formed me in the womb. And this, my dear sister and brother, is why I wanted to write this book: I have a story to tell you about that dream to become an artist. In the early days, becoming an artist brought many challenges to my life as one sector of the church did not understand the potential of art as an instrument of worship, evangelism, and emotional, physical, and spiritual healing, among other things. But I already had discovered in the Bible, through Bezalel, the *Poiesis Theou*...the Creator God, inexhaustible source of inspiration and artistic revelation.

God makes no distinction of person. He longs to reach all mankind. There are those who are sensitive to the beauty of a flower, and there are those who are excited to see a basketball game, read a philosophy book, or be a Brazilian jiu-jitsu black belt. And as the Creator God, He understands that some will be touched through the testimony of a boxer like Manny Pacquiao or the preaching by a pastor or an evangelist. But He knows better than anyone, because He made us, that there are others who will need theater, music, dance, cinema, visual arts—in short, the creative arts—to be touched and transformed by the power of God. I remember that once God whispered in my spirit, "As an artist, you will be able to reach places that others cannot because, usually, artists tend to be welcome everywhere," and so it has been. I feel grateful to God because I understand that he gave me the gift of art as an instrument to transform and literally save lives.

Art is a gift from God. I want you to discover and study the life of Bezalel, an artist called and supernaturally gifted by God. Here, you will find Bezalel's call, his divine mandate, his spiritual and artistic training, and the personal characteristics that made him, along with his work team, wise artists at heart. In the same way, God is calling you to transform your natural talents into supernatural so that you become like Bezalel, a wise artist at heart.

The Bible tells us in Ephesians 3:20–21, "Now to Him who is able to do exceedingly abundantly beyond all that we ask or imagine, according to the power that works in us, to Him be the glory in the church and in Christ Jesus throughout all generations, forever and ever. Amen." And I am a witness to this creative and artistic abundance of God.

DESIGN OF THE
TABERNACLE

CHAPTER 1

LET THEM MAKE ME A SANCTUARY

Beyond the Stone Tablets

> Let them make Me a sanctuary
> that I may dwell among them.
> Exodus 25:8

HISTORICAL BACKGROUND

Who was Bezalel? Who called him? When? Where? Why was he called? How is it that I have never heard of him before? These were some questions that came to my mind after my encounter with Bezalel in Exodus 31. This was the beginning of a search for answers, answers that, little by little, formed the biblical foundation of what I understand could be a theology of art. It did not take me long to realize that Bezalel was an artist set apart by God to carry out a monumental labor under challenging conditions. But we cannot understand the importance of Bezalel's vocation if we do not know nor understand the value and significance of the work to be done. I invite you to join me in discovering Bezalel's calling, which could very well be like yours since God calls us individually and by our names to carry out specific work for Him and His kingdom. I started to read, re-read, and compare over and over again different versions of chapter 31 of Exodus to see if they all said the same thing and if they offered additional details about Bezalel's calling. I still have this comparing habit.

The Bible says in Exodus 19:1, "In the third month after the children of Israel had gone forth out of the land of Egypt, on the same day they came into the Wilderness of Sinai." This place was well known by Moses since he encountered God there and received his calling to free the Israelites from the hand of the Egyptians. This place, known as Mount Horeb, is located in the desert of Sinai. For many Bible scholars, Mount Horeb is synonymous with Mount Sinai. For example, Adam Clarke[1] says in his Bible commentary that Horeb and Sinai were two peaks of the same mountain and that sometimes it was called Horeb and other times Sinai. Horeb was probably the early name of the mountain, which later was called "mountain of God" or "holy land" because God met Moses there. Mount Horeb is identified in Exodus 3:1 as the "mountain of God," and in Exodus 3:5, God said to Moses, "Do not approach here. Remove your sandals from your feet, for the place on which you are standing is holy ground." In Acts 7:30, it is called Mount Sinai: "an angel of the Lord appeared to him in the wilderness of Mount Sinai, in a flame of fire in a bush." And in Acts 7:33, it is confirmed as holy ground: "Then the Lord said to him, 'Take off the shoes from your feet, for the place where you are standing is holy ground."

To that "mountain of God" and "holy ground," God invited Moses to go and receive the tablets of stone, the law, the commandments that He had written to be taught to the people of Israel (Exodus 24:12). The Bible tells that Moses went amid a cloud and ascended the mountain and was with God forty days and forty nights (Exodus 24:18). One can see how the scenery is very particular. God invites Moses to the holy ground, a place that has been separated by Him, to talk and instruct Moses, and if the scenery was solemn, the drama that will be disclosed was even more so. The fact that Moses was with God on this mountain for forty days and forty nights, shows the importance of this meeting and its spiritual meaning. And again, one finds that the next time we see Moses with God at the mountain for forty days and forty nights, it is to intercede and literally plead for the lives of the people because they built a "molded image" (Deuteronomy 9:12). God told Moses, "Let Me alone, so that I may destroy them and blot out their name from under heaven" (Deuteronomy 9:14a). Therefore, these meetings with God for forty days and forty nights were transcendental for the life of the nation of Israel.

BUILD ME A SANCTUARY

During those forty days and forty nights, God not only gives Moses the tablets of stone, the law and commandments that He wrote, but He says, "Tell the children of Israel to bring Me an offering. From every man who gives willingly with his heart you shall receive My offering" (Exodus 25:2). The word "offering" in this passage comes from the Hebrew *terumah*,[2] and it is the first time that it is used. It is an offering, a gift, or a contribution that would be raised and elevated unto God, since a priest would have to elevate it and place it upon the altar, and it would consist of necessary things for the occasion. It was not an offering for Moses or the priests. God starts His petition by saying, "Bring Me an offering." Moses was just to be the collector of such an offering. God establishes certain requirements for this offering; it was a specific offering that had to be given voluntarily, without any pressure and from the heart; in other words, it had to be given with the right attitude. At the end of His petition to Moses, God says, "You shall receive My offering." It was not established how much to give, but it was established that each would give according to their generosity or their personal situation. The Lord was aware that this would not be a burden for the people, but a demonstration of love, thanksgiving, and obedience unto Him. The Lord not only promised deliverance from Egypt, but He also promised provision:

> "I will give this people favor in the sight of the Egyptians, and it will come to pass, that, when you go, you will not go empty-handed. But every woman will borrow of her

neighbor, and of her that sojourns in her house, articles of silver, and articles of gold, and clothing, and you will put them on your sons, and on your daughters—in this way you will plunder the Egyptians." (Exodus 3:21–22)

There are Bible scholars who say that even when the people of Israel were slaves for 400 years before leaving Egypt, they received retroactive pay for their hard labor there, specifically those who worked on the construction of Pithon and Raamses as storage cities for the pharaoh (Exodus 1:11). As a result of their obedience, God fulfilled His promise:

Now the children of Israel did according to the word of Moses, and they requested of the Egyptians articles of silver and articles of gold, and clothing. And the Lord gave the people favor in the sight of the Egyptians, so that they gave them *what they requested*. Thus they plundered the Egyptians. (Exodus12:35–36). God gives Moses the specifications of the kind of offering they would have to give. Let us remember that the Hebrew word used in this passage for "offering" is *terumah,* which would have consisted of things needed for the occasion, specific things, and God knew what was needed for the work that they would be doing:

This is the offering which you shall take from them: gold, silver, and bronze, blue, purple, scarlet, fine linen, goats' hair, rams' skins dyed red, porpoise skins, acacia wood, oil for the light, spices for anointing oil and for fragrant incense, onyx stones, and stones. (Exodus 25:3-7)

A classification of the list clearly shows that it was composed of metals, fabrics or textile material, skins, wood, oil and spices, and precious stones. There was a determined purpose with this list; it was a specific one, and they had to be very specific in their giving:

Metals: gold, silver, and brass

Fabrics:	blue, purple, scarlet, and fine linen
Skins:	goat hair, ram skins dyed in red, and `` porpoise' skins
Wood:	acacia
Oils:	olive oil
Spices:	pure myrrh, sweet cinnamon, sweet cane, cassia, sweet spices, stacte, onycha, galbanum, and sweet spices with pure frankincense (Exodus 30:23-34)
Stones:	onyx, sardius, topaz, carbuncle, emerald, sapphire, diamond, jacinth, agate, amethyst, beryl, and jasper (Exodus 28:9, 17--20)

Immediately after the petition of the offering, God continues to speak, telling Moses, "Let them make Me a sanctuary that I may dwell among them" (Exodus 25:8). I believe that when God spoke to Moses about giving him the law and the commandments, we could say that Moses felt glad because law brings order. The law is a guide and help to every leader. Nevertheless, construction work, no matter how simple, implies additional work. The people of Israel needed to be led to the Promised Land, and now they had to build the Tabernacle. Moses left with 600,000 men, and when counting women and children, as many as 1.5 or 2 million people. Exodus 12:38 also tells us, "A mixed multitude also went up with them along with flocks and herds, a large amount of livestock." This means that other Egyptian slaves also probably left with the Hebrews, following the example of the children of Israel by offering a lamb as a sacrifice because, whether there was a relationship with the Hebrew families or through them, they had seen the manifestation of God and they believed in Him. One can understand that this was a monumental job, leading numerous and diverse people with their animals, personal items, food, and other belongings, and now they had to build a sanctuary or tabernacle unto God. This mandate was an extraordinary one: to build a sanctuary, a holy place in the wilderness, where there were no facilities for water, food, or refreshing areas to rest at the end of a day's worth. Why in this place? Why in this historical moment?

Remember that when God created Adam and Eve, He placed them in the Garden of Eden. A garden is a place of farming where special care is given to plants, which generally are vegetables that nurture those who grow them, and usually, the place is complemented by flowers, fountains, and sculptures to add beauty to the place. It is a place that makes us feel good, and at the same time, it provides food for our nutrition and strength. In Genesis 3:8a, speaking about Adam and Eve, it says, "Then they heard the sound of the Lord God walking in the garden in the cool of the day." To me, this implies that God visited them often.

The garden of Eden was a place where there was communion between God and His greatest creation: a place where God placed man after his creation, gave a purpose to his life when He told him to take care and guard the garden and to name every living animal, and gave him instructions so that his life would be a prosperous one. But also set boundaries: " And the Lord God commanded the man, saying, 'Of every tree of the garden you may freely eat, but of the tree of the knowledge of good and evil you shall not eat, for in the day that you eat from it you will surely die'" (Genesis 2:16–17). Also, the garden was the place where God saw that man needed help, and He said, "It is not good that the man should be alone. I will make him a helper suitable for him" (Genesis 2:18).

Once Adam and Eve disobeyed God's commandment, the Word says, "Therefore the Lord God sent him out from the garden of Eden" (Genesis 3:23a). The special place where Adam and Eve met with God daily was no longer accessible to them. Adam and Eve not only lost the daily communion with their Creator, but they also lost the rest and life with a purpose that the relationship with God and the place provided for them. In Genesis 3:15, we can see the rebuke to the serpent, but we also have here the first occurrence of what is called the law of double reference.[3] This verse is commonly called the "Protevangelium" or the "first gospel proclamation."[4] Despite their disobedience, God gives them hope:

> The Lord God said to the serpent: "Because you have done this,
>
> You are cursed above all livestock,

and above every beast of the field;
you will go on your belly,
  and you will eat dust
  all the days of your life.
I will put enmity
  between you and the woman,
  and between your offspring and her offspring;
he will bruise your head,
  and you will bruise his heel." (Genesis 3:14–15)

Matthew Henry wrote in his *Commentary*:

A gracious promise is here made of Christ, as the deliverer of fallen man from the power of Satan. Though what was said was addressed to the serpent, yet it was said in the hearing of our first parents, who, doubtless, took the hints of grace here given them, and saw a door of hope opened to them, else the following sentence upon themselves would have overwhelmed them. Here was the dawning of the gospel day. No sooner was the wound given than the remedy was provided and revealed.[5]

And as a symbol of what He had already provided in His redemption plan, the Bible says, "The Lord God made garments of skins for both Adam and his wife and clothed them" (Genesis 3:21). To provide them with those tunics of skins, there had to be the shedding of blood; an animal was killed.

God does not forget His promises, and though more than two thousand years have gone by since the Hebrew nation left Egypt, the plan of redemption that God established still prevails. If we look a little further back, to almost two thousand years after God took Adam and Eve from the Garden, God speaks to Abraham:

Now the Lord said to Abram, "Go from your country, your family, and your father's house to the land that I will show you.

I will make of you a great nation;
  I will bless you
and make your name great,

so that you will be a blessing.
I will bless them who bless you
and curse him who curses you,
and in you all families of the earth
will be blessed." (Genesis 12:1–3)

The nation that comes out of Abraham is the one leaving Egypt under the leadership of Moses. The children of Israel remained in Egypt for 430 years, of which, for 400 years, they were slaves. When you are a slave, you are subject to your master, so maybe the children of Israel would know more of the Egyptians' gods than of their own God. But God takes them out of Egypt in a majestic way, in a way that would build memories and make them remember the stories that their ancestors may have told them about their God. They would be able to remember who Abraham was, and above all, they would realize that despite all the time that had gone by, God had not forgotten the promise He made:

> Then He said to Abram, "Know for certain that your descendants will live as strangers in a land that is not theirs, and they will be enslaved and mistreated for four hundred years. But I will judge the nation that they serve, and afterward they will come out with great possessions... On that same day the Lord made a covenant with Abram, saying, "To your descendants I have given this land, from the river of Egypt to the great Euphrates River." (Genesis 15:13–14, 18)

The people of Israel probably heard about how Joseph arrived in Egypt and became the instrument that would save the nation. Nevertheless, as time went by, they became slaves; but at the end of the exact time which God had told Abraham, they were freed, and they left with "plenty."

Once again, God speaks to Moses to give him instructions on what he needs to do. The Lord starts by reminding him what He has done with the people and why: "You have seen what I did to the Egyptians, and how I lifted you up on eagles' wings, and brought you to Myself" (Exodus 19:4). I understand that God wants to reestablish the daily communion that he had with the man and the woman in the Garden of Eden and to allow His presence to dwell amongst them, and He proposes the following, "Now therefore, if you will faithfully obey My voice and keep My covenant, then you shall be My special possession out of all the nations, for all the earth is Mine. And you will be to Me a kingdom of priests and a holy nation'" (Exodus 19:5–6).

The Tabernacle would be the visible manifestation of the presence of God amid His people. To the people who were taken out of Egypt, God says, "I lifted you up on eagles' wings, and brought you to Myself." I understand that in His desire to reestablish the daily communication that He once had in the garden with Adam and Eve, God designs the Tabernacle or meeting place. This would be like a "bridge" between God and man after the fall of Adam. This meeting place would be His sanctuary, His habitation. It would be the visible house of God. The sanctuary would be a place for God to inhabit and a witness of the constant presence of God with the people of Israel. It would be the place where the people would come to gather with their God to worship Him, a place of prayer and adoration, a place where the people would come to present their petitions and receive their answers. It would be the place where the Lord would reveal His will to His people, where He would put His name and consecrate symbols of His presence, like the Ark of the Covenant.

The presence of God in the Tabernacle would be a sign of His grace and mercy towards the children of Israel. It would be the public demonstration that God was with them to protect them, govern them, judge them, and bless them. It would be a place that would show the way towards that promise of redemption made at the Garden of Eden to Adam and Eve. As it is said by the apostle Paul in Hebrews, "But Christ, when He came as a High Priest of the good things to come, by a greater and more perfect tabernacle, not made with hands, that is to say, not of this creation" (Hebrews 9:11). Because people lived in tents, this sanctuary would be a gigantic tent. The tents could be set up and taken down easily, which allowed both the people and the presence of God to move together.

I believe that the implications of the job to be done are enormous. It is not a common petition. We are talking about God, the Creator of Heaven and Earth, whom Moses knew from the burning bush (Exodus 3). The Bible says that when the main leaders of Israel, Aaron, Nadab, and Abiu, ascended to the mountain with Moses, "they saw the God of Israel, and under His feet there was something like a paved work of sapphire stone as clear as the sky itself" (Exodus 24:10). I believe that Moses had a pretty good idea of the majesty of God, and it is the first time that God speaks about having a place for Himself. Therefore, I imagine the challenge and the thoughts that went through Moses's mind during those moments: how was he to design a place for the Lord? But it was not Moses who would design the Tabernacle.

Notes:

[1]Adam Clarke, *Commentary on the Bible*, https://sacred-texts.com/bib/cmt/clarke/exo003.htm.

[2]James Strong, LL.D., S.T.D., *The New Strong's Expanded Exhaustive Concordance of the Bible*, (Nashville: Thomas Nelson, 2010), 301.

[3]Finis Jennings Dake, *Dake's Annotated Reference Bible*, (Georgia; Dake Publishing, Inc., 2014), 93.

[4]https://www.christiancourier.com/articles/1571-crushing-the-serpents-head-the-meaning-of-genesis-3-15.

[5]https://www.biblegateway.com/resources/matthew-henry/Gen.3.14-Gen.3.15.

CHAPTER 2

THE TABERNACLE
Design and Specifications

See that you make them according to their
pattern which was shown to you on the mountain.
Exodus 25:40

THE LORD WILL BE THE DESIGNER

It is interesting to note that one usually only associates the encounter between the Lord with Moses at the mountain for forty days and forty nights with the handing over of the tablets of stone and the law. Regarding the details that are given for the Tabernacle, furniture, and accessories, it seems to me that God spent a great part of the time instructing Moses about it, explaining the design and details, clearing out any doubts, and identifying who could do the work and how He would prepare them for the project. Even more, He was probably emphasizing over and over that the Tabernacle would be a reflection, a prototype of He who was to come. Therefore, Moses had to follow all the instructions verbatim. Moses was responsible to the Lord for the work to be done.

I would love to have been behind a rock to hear about all the details, and even more, to see the design of the Tabernacle created by God. However, the apostle Paul, in 2 Timothy 3:16a, tells us, "All Scripture is inspired by God," and thanks to that divine inspiration, today we have a reliable report of what happened in the meeting between the Lord and Moses that serves as a guide to help us understand why and how the Tabernacle was built and what it tells us today. Let us see, then, what needed to be done.

THE LORD WOULD SHOW THE DESIGN

In Exodus 25:9, the Lord said to Moses, "According to all that I show you—the pattern of the tabernacle and the pattern of all its furniture—you shall make it just so." In other words, the main architect and designer would be God himself. This design includes the Tabernacle and all its furniture and accessories. From Exodus 25:10 all the way to Exodus 30:39, we can find an account of what God showed Moses was needed to be done. The description includes the different furniture and accessories, specifications as to different materials, colors, and measures, and even the techniques of how to build them and the purpose of each one.

In other words, the designer and principal architect would be God. I imagine that any questions as to how the sanctuary would be built ceased when God said, "According to what I show you, you will do." The Lord showed Moses the design of the Tabernacle with the necessary details for it to be successful, "See that you make them according to their pattern which was shown to you on the mountain" (Exodus 25:40). And this expression, or variations of it, is repeated twenty times.

THE ARK OF THE TESTIMONY

Let us examine how the Ark of the Testimony was to be built (Exodus 25:10–22), which is the first piece of furniture mentioned. In this description of the construction of the Ark of the Testimony, three important aspects are emphasized: the measurements of the ark, the specifications of the materials to be used, and lastly, the purpose for the ark.

The Ark of the Testimony had two parts: the ark and the cover with its two cherubim.

Measurements:
- Length 3.67 feet (1.12 meters)
- Width 2.23 feet (68 centimeters)
- Height 2.23 feet (68 centimeters)

Specifications:
- The ark would be built out of acacia wood.
- It would be covered with gold on the inside and outside.
- The top of the ark would be surrounded by a gold cornice.
- It had to have four rings cast in pure gold, one ring on each corner, two rings on one side, and two rings on the other.
- It would have two acacia wood rods coated with gold.
- The rods would pass through the rings on the sides of the ark so that it could be carried. The rods would need to be kept through the rings of the ark at all times.

Purpose:
- "And you shall put into the ark of the testimony which I shall give you" (Exodus 25:16). Hebrews 9:4 tells us the testimony that was placed inside the ark: "It contained Manna, Aaron's Rod budded, and the tables of the covenant."

THE COVER OF GOLD WITH THE TWO CHERUBIM

Measurements:
- Length 3.67 feet (1.12 meters)
- Width 2.23 feet (68 centimeters)
Specifications:
- The cover of the ark would be made of pure gold.

- The cover, with the two cherubim, was to be made in one piece (which indicates how the cover was to be constructed).
- The cover would be placed on top of the ark.
- The ark was to be placed in the Holy of Holies.
- The cherubim would be made out of pure gold
- One cherub would be at one extreme of the cover, and the other at the opposite extreme of the cover.
- The wings of the cherubim would extend up in a way that the topping would be covered with them as they faced each other. The faces of the cherubim would look down at the cover.

Purpose:
- And there I will meet with you, and I will commune with you from above the mercy seat, from between the two cherubim which are upon the Ark of the Testimony, all of the things which I will give you in commandment for the children of Israel. (Exodus 25:22)

If we observe carefully, these pieces would require knowledge in the area of joinery and metals. Even more, the fact that the top cover and the two cherubim would have to be made one piece with a hammer indicates a highly developed artistic skill level. I challenge you to get a hammer and bullion of gold and start hammering to see if you can get the top cover with two beautiful cherubim like they did.

The Ark of the Testimony is just one example of the work to be done, but it makes us understand the seriousness of Bezalel's calling and of the ones who collaborated with him. One can easily sum up in one or two sentences his work without realizing all the effort and discipline he needed to carry it out. I recognize that in the transcendental time that we live in today, where art is being restored to its original purpose, understanding Bezalel's calling and his artistic, technical, and, above all, spiritual preparation for the job is essential for us artists of the 21st century.

WORK OF A SKILLED ARTIST

(Note: For the complete list of the work to be done, with all its specifications, see APPENDIX A).

As you have already noticed, the construction of the Tabernacle needed, above all, obedience. The instructions needed to be followed without altering them. There was also a need for high skills in areas that were extremely diverse, from the cutting of the acacia wood bars to the sewing and embroidering. Maybe the knowledge of the construction was not a challenge for the Israelites due to the time they'd spent working in Egypt. Nevertheless, now they were in the desert, and conditions had drastically changed. Some pieces required artistic skills, like the creation of the ark with its two cherubim and the chandelier made out of pure gold, all of one piece.

The project required knowledge about the different materials to be used, like the metals, wood, fabric, precious stones, oil, and spices, among many others. It needed knowledge about measurements, since there was wood to be cut according to specific measures and furniture to be built, and the designs that God had shown to Moses needed to be made without straying from the instructions given by God. To be able to build the top cover of the ark with its cherubim on one piece as God indicated, the builder needed knowledge about proportions, colors, and perspectives. Knowledge was required of how to make the fabric, prepare the fine linen, prepare the colors, and dye the fabrics, how to preserve the skins, how to cut the bars, to melt gold and silver and coat the wood with them. Knowledge was needed to properly interpret the designs of the holy garments of the priests and make them. Knowledge was needed in sewing, weaving, embroidery, carving wood, and engraving stones and metals and also to make the oil and the incense for the altar.

There was a need for people knowledgeable in engineering and architecture to understand the design and assembly of the Tabernacle to be able to build it so that it would stand firm even in the hostile conditions of the desert. At the same time, it would have to be a mobile Tabernacle, as it would have to move or camp under

God's command. Everything had to be made skillfully. God repeats to Moses that the work requires special skills: "It should be of cunning work," or, as in some other versions, "of skillful work" (Exodus 26:31, 36; 28:6, 8, 15). In other words, it had to be made to perfection; the artists needed to know what they were doing.

We have seen how, on the way to the promised land, God gave Moses this great work. And in the same way that God called and prepared Moses to deliver the people out of slavery from Egypt, He prepared the man who would be responsible for carrying out the construction of the Tabernacle, along with those who would assist.

One of my purposes for writing this book is that the Bible's approach to the arts serves as a model for the development of contemporary art projects, and Bezalel's calling is a wonderful example to follow. The Lord had no difficulty showing Moses a unique and beautiful design. With the ark and the mercy seat, we have seen an example of how specific God can be in revealing a project or an idea. He showed the design, the materials, how to do it, its purpose, and even the name of the project. We understand, then, that God, in these times, can do the same with us and show us projects that impact nations. If he did it with Moses, he can do it with us also, "for there is no partiality with God" (Romans 2:11).

CHAPTER 3

CALLED BY HIS NAME
God Called an Artist

> Now the Lord spoke to Moses, saying:
> See, I have called by name Bezalel the son
> of Uri, the son of Hur, of the tribe of Judah.
> Exodus 31:1–2

BEZALEL

Every plan from God is admirable and perfect and takes into consideration all aspects of the work to be done. God indicated to Moses that an offering had to be collected pro-Tabernacle, and He gave him the design for it, but who would complete this work? We know that the Tabernacle was beyond a simple tent or group of selected rocks placed one on top of the other to form an altar. I figure that for a second, Moses saw himself cutting some wood or melting metals. The Lord knew that Moses was equipped to face Pharaoh and that he was also prepared to govern and lead the people of Israel, but he was not prepared to construct the Tabernacle and all of its furniture and accessories.

Aware that God is our Creator, King David tells us, "Your hands have made me and fashioned me" (Psalms 119:73a), and he continues in more detail:

> You brought my inner parts into being;
>   You wove me in my mother's womb.
> I will praise you, for You made me with fear and wonder;
>   marvelous are Your works,
>   and You know me completely.
> My frame was not hidden from You
>   when I was made in secret,
> and intricately put together in the lowest parts of the earth.
>   Your eyes saw me unformed,
> yet in Your book
>   all my days were written,
>   before any of them came into being. (Psalms 139:13–16)

It is God who qualifies us even before our birth. An example of this is the testimony that is narrated to us by the prophet Jeremiah about his calling:

> Now the word of the Lord came to me, saying,
>
> "Before I formed you in the womb I knew you;
>   and before you were born I sanctified you,
>   and I ordained you a prophet to the nations." (Jeremiah 1:4–5)

Since it is God who made us "and not we ourselves" (Psalm 100:3), He knows exactly who He calls and the specific work that one can do. When someone was needed to deliver the people of Israel from Egypt, God called Moses. He came up with an excuse like, "O my Lord, I am not eloquent, neither before nor since You have spoken to Your servant. But I am slow of speech, and of a slow tongue" (Exodus 4:10), and the Lord replied, "Is not Aaron the Levite your brother? I know that he can speak well. And also, he comes out to meet you, and when he sees you, he will be glad in his heart. You shall speak to him and put the words in his mouth, and

I will be with your mouth, and with his mouth, and will teach you what you must do" (Exodus 4:14–15).

It has been demonstrated that even when we think that we do not have what it is required to do the work, God has already thought about the solution to what we believe to be obstacles to accomplish the divine mandate. God wanted the children of Israel to construct a sanctuary for Him, and someone special was needed for this special work. Once again, we see how God already has the person prepared, "Now the Lord spoke to Moses, saying: See, I have called by name Bezalel..." (Exodus 31:1–2). If we would closely analyze the sentence, the action happened in the past, but it keeps its relation to the present: "I have called." For this moment, for this work that needed to be done, "I have called Bezalel by name." The person had already been called, appointed, and separated by God. In other words, the Lord told him, and here, I again use my poetic license:

> Look, Moses, don't worry. Keep in mind that I have specifically chosen Bezalel to do the job. I do not expect you to do this on your own. Even more, I hope you do not touch anything of this work because, for that, I called and separated Bezalel. Just make sure that everything is done as it was shown to you on the mountain.

Just like with Moses, God conferred upon Bezalel a particular honor. He called him by his name, and He called him to do a transcendental job. Bezalel was not a Levite or a great warrior, but God called him to play a crucial role in the construction of the first sanctuary. He called him by his own name. And, I wonder, what is the importance of being called by name? Your name is closely linked to your person. It is usually the first question asked to you and the first thing you receive at birth and with which you are set apart from others. According to the Hebrew tradition, there is a spiritual connection between the name and the person who carries it. For the Hebrews, to mention someone's name was to seek their presence.[1] In the Bible, it is a great honor when God calls someone by name because this indicates that he has been chosen for a specific reason, to perform a particular task or mission.

Examples are Moses (Exodus 3:4), the prophet Samuel (1 Samuel 3:1–10), and the apostle Paul (Acts 9:4).

Another interesting fact is that the Scriptures say that the Lord spoke to Moses face to face, and on more than one occasion, He told him, "I know you by name" (Exodus 33:17). In this verse, the Hebrew word for "know" is *yada*,[2] and it means to be known by experience through direct observation or firsthand experience. No one told God about Moses; He knew Moses intimately; He knew him through firsthand information obtained by direct observation.

If we go to the New Testament, Jesus had direct knowledge about each one of His disciples. For example, when God calls Peter, He tells him, "'You are Simon the son of John. You shall be called Cephas' (which means Peter)" (John 1:42). And, when Jesus sees Nathaniel, He says, "Here is an Israelite indeed, in whom is no guile." Nathanael says to Him, "How do You know me?" Jesus answers him, "Before Philip called you, when you were under the fig tree, I saw you" (John 1:47–48). If one studies the calling of apostle Paul, which happened after the resurrection and ascension of Jesus to Heaven, one can see that even when Saul was persecuting the church, he was called by his name:

> Saul, still breathing out threats and murder against the disciples of the Lord, went to the high priest, and requested letters from him to the synagogues of Damascus, so that if he found any there of the Way, either men or women, he might bring them bound to Jerusalem. As he went he drew near Damascus, and suddenly a light from heaven shone around him. He fell to the ground and heard a voice saying to him, "Saul, Saul, why do you persecute Me?"
>
> He said, "Who are You, Lord?"
>
> The Lord said, "I am Jesus, whom you are persecuting. It is hard for you to kick against the goads." (Acts 9:1–5).

And as with others chosen or separated for a mission, there is always a purpose behind it. For example, when Jesus speaks to Ananias by vision and sends him to pray for Saul, in the face of Ananias's logical fear, Jesus tells him, "But the Lord said to him,

'Go your way. For this man is a chosen vessel of Mine, to bear My name before the Gentiles and their kings, and before the sons of Israel'" (Acts 9:15).

To me, one of the most peculiar things with Bezalel's calling is that God speaks to Moses about it. Usually, the Word tells us, God calls the person directly: "So God said to Noah, 'The end of all flesh is come before Me... Make an ark of cypress wood'" (Genesis 6:13–14); "Now the Lord said to Abram, 'Go from your country, your family'" (Genesis 12:1); to Isaac, he says, "I am the God of Abraham your father" (Genesis 26:24); He said unto Jacob, "Arise, go up to Bethel" (Genesis 35:1); and to Moses, the Bible says, "God called to him from out of the midst of the bush and said, 'Moses, Moses'" (Exodus 3:4). However, this is the first time that I find in the Bible that God tells another person, in this case, Moses: "See I have called Bezalel by his name." This right away makes me think of a code of honor or a spiritual protocol.

God established an order or protocol when He called Bezalel. According to the dictionary, protocol is the "set of rules and ceremonials that should be followed on certain occasions and with certain personalities."[3] This has reminded me of the law of submission and the law of delegated authority. In the law of submission, loyalty is owed to the leader or to the person in highest authority over us: "Obey your leaders and submit to them, for they watch over your souls as those who must give an account. Let them do this with joy and not complaining, for that would not be profitable to you" (Hebrews 13:17). In this case, Bezalel owed loyalty and obedience to Moses in the same way that Moses submitted to the Lord.

In delegated authority, God authorized Bezalel, through his calling, to be the artist and constructor of the Tabernacle, and Moses the superintendent or manager. Through his calling, Bezalel got the authority to act independently but within the limits prescribed by Moses (which he received from God). At the same time, Moses did not give up his authority, but shared some of it with Bezalel so he could complete the responsibility entrusted to him. This is why, after the job was completed, Moses had to respond to God because the work had to follow the pattern of the Tabernacle and its furniture that had been shown to Moses on the mountain. So,

Moses had to be sure that Bezalel did his job according to all that the Lord had commanded him.

God continued to talk to Moses and specified not only the name of Bezalel but also his heritage: "the son of Uri, the son of Hur, of the tribe of Judah" (Exodus 31:2). Not only did God call him by his name, but He identified his father, his grandfather, and the tribe he came from. When I read the verses for the first time, I thought about how specific God was in not only calling Bezalel by his name, but also identifying his grandfather and his father so that there would not be any doubt as to who the person selected was. But now I understand that there is a deeper message that God wants us to discover, since Bezalel's genealogy appears five times in the Bible:

> See, I have called by name Bezalel the son of Uri, the son of Hur, of the tribe of Judah. (Exodus 31:2)

> Moses said to the children of Israel: See, the Lord has called by name Bezalel the son of Uri, the son of Hur, of the tribe of Judah. (Exodus 35:30)

> Bezalel, the son of Uri the son of Hur of the tribe of Judah, made all that the Lord commanded Moses. (Exodus 38:22)

> Hur became the father of Uri, and Uri became the father of Bezalel.

> 1 (Chronicles 2:20)

> And the bronze altar that Bezalel the son of Uri, the son of Hur, had made was set before the tabernacle of the Lord. And Solomon and the assembly sought it out *to seek the* Lord. (2 Chronicles 1:5)

This repetition of Bezalel's genealogy makes me understand its importance. No information in the Bible was set down by chance or to expand the chapter because the editor found it too short. It was set down because God, through his Spirit, wanted to point something out. The Holy Scriptures tell us, " It is the glory of God to conceal a thing, but the honor of kings is to search out a matter"

(Proverbs 25:2). The Hebrew word for "scrutinize" is *chaqar*,[4] and it means "to discern, to examine intimately, to discover." It is to go beyond the obvious, to open the door of the unknown and inquire, ask, and investigate. And that is what I want to do. I will continue removing the veil.

The story of Bezalel[5] is a fascinating one; his name means "under the shadow of God,"[5] that is, "under the protection of the almighty." This idea of shadow as protection appears in Psalm 91:1: "He who dwells in the shelter of the Most High shall abide under the shadow of the Almighty." And we also see it in Psalm 121:5–6: "The Lord is your guardian; the Lord is your shade at your right hand. The sun shall not harm you during the day, nor the moon during the night." Bezalel, as the artist in charge of the construction of the Tabernacle, was to be under the shadow and protection of God. And not only that, but a look at Psalm 63:7 tells us about an intimate fellowship with God in addition to divine protection: "Because You have been my help, therefore in the shadow of Your wings I will rejoice." Bezalel, as the artist in charge of the Tabernacle, was going to be under the shadow and protection of God.

His father went by the name of Uri,[6] which means "light," and his grandfather Hur,[7, 8] which means "noble, splendorous, white." Hur, the father of Bezalel, was with Moses and Aaron when Joshua went out to fight against Amalec: "So Joshua did as Moses had said to him and fought against Amalek. And Moses, Aaron, and Hur went up to the top of the hill. Now when Moses held up his hand, Israel prevailed, but when he let down his hand, Amalek prevailed" (Exodus 17:10–11). Hur was certainly a nobleman, and besides accompanying Moses and Aaron, he held Moses's arms, along with Aaron, when they were tired: "But Moses' hands became heavy. So they took a stone, and put it under him, and he sat on it. And Aaron and Hur supported his hands, one on one side, and the other on the other side. And his hands were steady until the going down of the sun" (Exodus 17:12). And when the Lord asked Moses to come up to the mountain to receive the tablets of stone and the law, Moses told the elders, "Wait for us in this place until we return to you. Aaron and Hur are with you. Whoever has any matters of dispute let him come to them" (Exodus 24:14).

Again, we see Hur taking over, along with Aaron, a position of leadership and of service.

The *Rabbinic literature*[9] and some biblical commentators, such as Matthew Henry, identify Caleb as one of the twelve spies and as Bezalel's great-grandfather based on the following biblical text: "Now Azubah died, and Caleb took Ephrath as a wife. She bore Hur for him. Hur became the father of Uri, and Uri became the father of Bezalel" (1 Chronicles 2:19–20). According to rabbinical sources, Caleb, the son of Hezron (1 Chronicles 2:18–20), is identified as Caleb, the son of Jephone (Numbers 13:6). The epithet "Jefone" (meaning "departed") was given because he rejected the sinful intention of the other spies who advised people not to go to the promised land. However, other biblical historians emphasize that Caleb, the son of Hezron, and Caleb, the son of Jefone, are two different people.

On the other hand, Flavio Josefo, a Jewish historian who lived during the same time of the apostles, wrote in his book *Jewish Antiquities*[10] that Mary, Moses' sister, was married to Hur, thus becoming Bezalel's great-grandmother and making Moses something like a great-granduncle.[8] And according to the Hebrew tradition, it is said that Bezalel was called by God when he was around thirteen years of age.

Bezalel was born in Egypt about 35 centuries ago. He belonged to the tribe of Judah. Being the most numerous and powerful, the tribe of Judah was the tribe that marched forward when the nation went to war (Numbers 10:14). Judah in Hebrew is *Yehudah*[11] and derives from the word *yadah*,[12] which means praise.

Bezalel was called to be in charge of the construction of the Tabernacle, specifically to deal directly with the works in metal, wood, and rock: "to devise artistic works for work with gold, with silver, and with bronze, and in the cutting of stones for settings, and in carving of wood, to work in all manner of craftsmanship" (Exodus 31:4–5). Bezalel was to be the artist and constructor of the Tabernacle, to create designs, work the metals, as in gold and silver, precious stones, and wood. If we analyze the necessary skills and knowledge needed to realize the construction of the Tabernacle, we notice that they would have to have been exceptional. Without any doubt, Bezalel was an artist! What? God dared call an artist to lead the construction of the Tabernacle? His Sanctuary? The place where He said His presence would dwell?

When we study the design of the Tabernacle, the furniture, accessories, and garments, we can see the need for diversified artistic skills. For example, inventing designs is a creative activity. To work with metals such as gold, silver, and brass, it is necessary to have, among other things, the technical ability and skill of a smelter, sculptor, artisan, and jeweler. To work and mount precious stones on another material requires the skills of a silver master. For example, the two onyx jewels on the priests' garments would be mounted on gold finishing. To work with wood and make the furniture of the Tabernacle, one would have to be an excellent woodcarver.

So far, what I have discovered about Bezalel seems wonderful to me, an artist called by God to build a sanctuary for the God of Heaven. And that sanctuary would be a reflection of the heavenly sanctuary. But an encounter with another Jewish artist, or perhaps a contemporary Bezalel, would open new horizons for me.

THE LAW OF BEZALEL OR THE LAW OF CREATIVITY

My encounter with the work of Edward Ephraim Kalish was unexpected. While working on the new material that I was going to add to Bezalel's book for its second edition, I discovered the documentary *Bezalel: Son of Light*. I immediately got a copy. It confirms many of my findings, but what struck me most was reading Kalish's biography. I found several points where we agree, especially regarding the Bible and art. After an email with his wife, she confirmed once again the majesty of the God I serve.

Edward Ephraim Kalish was born in Kazan, Russia, in 1962. He is an architect, graphic artist, sculptor, and filmmaker. He has a master's degree in architecture from the Kazan Academy of Architecture, where, for several years, he taught painting, graphics, architecture, and sculpture. He also studied design and graphic art in Riga (Letonia). His wife, Ivetta, is also a graduate of the Academy of Architecture. His parents are Jewish, but according to Kalish, his father is a communist, which explains why he grew up in a secular environment and unaware of his Jewish heritage. In 1993, he discovered that the God of Abraham, Isaac, and Jacob was also his God. And according to him, this revelation changed his life. In 1996, Kalish and his wife emigrated from the former Soviet Union to Haifa, Israel.

Once God entered his life, Kalish faced, as many of us have, the decision of whether to continue with the arts or not. In his biography, written by Martin Shoub, author of the book *To the Jew First: The Formation of One New Man*, Kalish describes the beginning of his relationship with God and art:

> Ephraim was forced to ask some deep questions of himself and of his God. He had always been an artist of one sort or another and was at a crossroads of identity and purpose. Ephraim: "As a young believer I was zealous for God and was even willing to give up art for His sake. I wanted to know what God thought about art, not just as an intellectual exercise – it was a practical issue. I didn't know what else I could do. How else would I live?" Ephraim began a serious study of what the Bible says about art and artists. From Ephraim's experience in religious circles, both Jewish and Christian, he saw how religious institutions had denigrated the role of artists in society. But his study of scripture produced a different conclusion. As with every good and perfect gift, art was God's idea in the first place.[13]

And just as God directed my steps to have an encounter with Bezalel, the God that Kalish had barely discovered also directed his steps to meet Bezalel. What he discovered; he talks about in his documentary *Bezalel: Son of Light*.[14]

From the beginning of the documentary, Kalish establishes God as the Creator God. In his discussion of the definition of what Jewish art is, he begins by quoting Numbers 23:9b: "The people will dwell alone and will not be counted among the nations." According to Kalish, "The people of Israel are not from this world, so the art of these people is not from this world either. This art has a heavenly source. It is directed to the heavens and there is a name that represents that art, and that name is Bezalel."

I found his theory fascinating because we, the Gentiles, as Galatians 3:29 says, "If you are Christ's, then you are Abraham's seed, and heirs according to the promise." Therefore, we are not from this world, either, and our art also has a heavenly source. In John 17:16, Jesus confirms this through his prayer: "They are not of the world even as I am not of the world."

Kalish discovers that the law of creativity is demonstrated and explained in the name and genealogy of Bezalel, and this has the same importance for artists as the laws of purity and sacrifices have for priests. As I noted earlier, the name Bezalel means "in the shadow of God, under the protection of God." However, Kalish helps us see other aspects in the name of Bezalel and his genealogy. To do this, he resorts to the Jewish tradition of interpreting the Holy Scriptures, known as the Midrash, and to the etymology or study of the origin of words. It is important to note that the Hebrew language is very rich in symbolism. Each letter represents a number, a phonetic sound, and an image. Almost all Hebrew words are based on root letters called *shoresh* ("root"). For example, the root *Tsade Lamed* consists of two letters: *Tsade* and *Lamed*.

In the name Bezalel, we find the root *Tsade Lamed*. Bezalel's name means "in the shadow of God." But when we study it from an etymological perspective, its meaning expands or deepens. The following words have the same etymological root as Bezalel: *tsel, tselem,* and *tseeloom.*

Tsel	means shadow, coverage, protection
Tselem	means image
Tseeloom	means copy / photo

Kalish points out that the name of Bezalel is a combination of:

Tsel (shadow) + *Tselem* (image) + *El* (God).

He understands that we have been created in the shadow and image of God. Genesis 1:26 tells us, "Let us make man in our image, after our likeness." Then God said, Let us make man in our image." We understand, therefore, that we have been made "in the image of God," which translates into Hebrew as *B'tselem Elohim.* In

35

B'tselem Elohim, we see one of the words (*tselem*) that form the name of Bezalel. Therefore, we can say that Bezalel means "image of God."

It is interesting to note that in *Bezalel: Redeeming a Renegade Creation* (2015), by Christ John Otto, *b'tselem Elohim* appears translated as" little creator." This makes a lot of sense since we have been created in the image of God and God's first order, after blessing humankind, was to "be fruitful and multiply" (Genesis 1:28). Chris John Otto emphasizes that the "little creators" are the shadows of God Himself. He expands the concept of Bezalel as the shadow of God when he introduces the Jewish philosopher Philo, who lived during the time of the apostle Paul. Philo translates the name Bezalel into Greek as *en skia Theou,* and *skia* means "replica of." Bezalel, instead of being "in the shadow of someone" becomes "the shadow of the original." Therefore, Bezalel is the reflection of God.

For Kalish, a man created in the image of God is a man with the ability and the need to create, and as a result of this similarity, the artist must reflect the glory of God. This is consistent with the Greek translation of the name Bezalel (*en skia Theou*): reflection of God.

God gave a great gift to man, Kalish emphasizes, and it is to be filled by the inspiration of God so that, in his creativity, he can be like his Creator and, in this way, can reveal the great power and glory of God. And in the same way that our shadows follow our bodies and are never separated from them, creativity must be determined by the law of the eternal God, and the artist must be faithful to his Creator and follow him. Therefore, in the artist following his Creator, we see fulfilled what Psalm 91:1 tells us: "He who dwells in the shelter of the Most High shall abide under the shadow of the Almighty." That is, we will be under God's coverage and protection.

Another word with the root *Tsade Lamed* is *Tseeloom,* which means "copy/photo." Kalish makes an analogy here where he compares the heart with photographic paper. Photo paper is sensitive to light. Similarly, Kalish recommends, our heart must be sensitive to the light of God. By being sensitive to the light of God, our Creator can create things through us. The call of man is to represent and reflect the greatness of the Creator of the universe. Therefore, Bezalel means "in the shadow and image of God," someone created to represent and reflect the greatness of a Creator God. We create to honor God because He created us in His image. We honor the Creator God with our art.

Bezalel, son of Uri. Uri means "light" and comes from the Hebrew "ori." "Uri" is also a compound word, where the U, derived from the letter *yud*, represents the name of the Lord. Therefore, we can say, "Uri, light of the Lord." Kalish tells us that our ability to see depends on the light. And we see things in one way or another depending on what kind of light we have. For example, the light that God created on the first day, Kalish explains, is a different light from sunlight or infrared light. He identifies the light created by God on the first day of creation with the light that David mentions in Psalm 119:105, "Your word is a lamp to my feet and a light to my path." Therefore, according to Kalish, the most important of all talents is the ability to see, to receive the light of God's Word, to be sensitive to receive God's inspiration. And this ability to see correctly is directly connected to our relationship with God: "in your light we will see light" (Psalm 36:9b). In order to see, we need light, but the most important light is the light of God, the light of His Word.

Kalish understands that light is necessary to produce a shadow and reproduce an image on a light-sensitive surface. Therefore, he concludes that the shadow is born from the light; and Bezalel, in the shadow of God, is born of Uri, which means "light of God." In this, he is very emphatic when he reiterates that to create something for the Lord and obey His mandate, the artist, by necessity, has to be born from the light of God. In this way, the artist can reflect the light and glory of God in his art because his heart is sensitive to the light of the Messiah and can create under the inspiration of God. Bezalel, therefore, is a child of the light of the Lord.

According to Kalish, Bezalel is the son of Uri, son of the first light, which reflects the purity and holiness of the Creator. "Holiness" can be defined as total dedication to someone or something and complete separation from that which is unclean. Bezalel's grandfather's name speaks to us of purity.

"Hur" means "pure," "white," and therefore expresses purity and holiness. Kalish emphasizes several times throughout his presentation the need for purity as an essential condition for the artist to stand before the Lord since the Bible speaks of its value: Bezalel, son of Hur, son of purity and holiness. Kalish, therefore, believes that the artist must have the same purity and holiness of the Creator and must belong to Him completely. Only, in this case, the artist will be called Hur's son. And I say, glory to God for Jesus Christ, who redeemed us and sanctified us!

Bezalel, son of Uri, son of Hur, of the tribe of Judah. According to Kalish, an etymological study of the word *Yehudah* (Judah) shows that it can be interpreted as "he who bears the power of the name of the Lord over him." We also find that the word "praise" is hidden in the name of Judah. In short, Kalish tells us that *Yehudah* is "he who thanks the Lord and worships him." This is the secret of the power of the name Judah.

The emblem of the tribe of Judah is the lion. We find this emblem in Genesis 49:9 and in Numbers 24:9. It is a symbol of strength, courage, and royalty. Kalish understands that the attributes of Judah must be in Jewish art and, consequently, the artist. This art is like the king's words: people pay attention to him. He is powerful, like a lion. It carries the power of God and contains the name of God. Exalt His name among the nations.

According to Kalish, we could summarize Bezalel's genealogy as follows:

> Bezalel, son of Uri, is a shadow born from the light of the Creator. Son of Hur, he belongs totally to the one who gave him life and dedicated himself completely to Him. The son of Judah is called to emphasize His glory. Only the artist who loves God and respects his laws is able to fulfill the "do it for me" commitment, which means "make your art for me." Only the artist committed to God can do something creative in the presence of the Lord.

In conclusion, summarizing what we have discovered so far about Bezalel, we could say:

- As artists, we are under the shadow and special protection of the Most High.
- As artists, we are shadows born from the light of the Creator.
- As artists, we are small creators. We are the reflections of a Creator God.
- As artists, we recognize God and His Word as our light.
- As artists, our lives must be completely dedicated to God.
- As artists, we belong to the tribe of Judah (praise), called to emphasize the
  glory of God.
- Only the artist who loves God and respects His laws can fulfill the commitment to create art for the glory of God.

OHOLIAB

As we have already noticed, the construction of the Tabernacle was not going to be an easy task. Oholiab[15] was to be Bezalel's assistant: "And behold I have given with him Oholiab, the son of Ahisamach, of the tribe of Dan" (Exodus 31:6). His name means "tabernacle or tent of my father."[16] The name Ahisamach, his father, means "helping brother or supporter."[15] Oholiab was from the tribe of Dan, the last tribe of the camp. He was an expert in textiles and, among other things, "an engraver, and a cunning workman, and an embroiderer in blue and purple, and in scarlet and fine linen" (Exodus 38:23). In other words, Bezalel's assistant would be another artist. He would complement Bezalel's skills and talents.

THE TABERNACLE

We have seen from Exodus 25:10 all the way to Exodus 30:38 a detailed description of the Tabernacle, its furniture and accessories, and the priest's garments. Once again, after God tells Moses that Bezalel, Oholiab, and others of "wise heart" had been called for the construction task, we see again another brief and specific list of "things to be done" concerning the construction of the Tabernacle. I understand that the Spirit inspires the author of Exodus to emphasize the importance of these things to be done:

- The Tabernacle
- The Ark of Testimony
- The cover over the Ark of Testimony
- All the vases of the Tabernacle
- The table with the vases
- The chandelier and all its vases
- The Altar of Perfume
- The Altar of the Holocaust and all its vases
- The fountain and the basin
- The garments of service, the holy garments of Aaron, the priest, and the garments for his sons
- The anointing oil and the aromatics for the sanctuary

And again, He says that they have to do it "according to all that I have commanded you" (Exodus 31:11b).

TO THE WISE HEARTED

The calling was not just for Bezalel and Oholiab. The Lord knew that the task was big and complicated and would be done in the middle of the desert. Besides, I understand that when God calls us and gives us a mission, He places people next to us who will help us complete the project. God says to Moses, "And thou shalt speak unto all that are wise hearted, whom I have filled with the spirit of wisdom, that they may make Aaron's garments to consecrate him, that he may minister unto me in the priest's office" (Exodus 28:3, KJV). I love the King James Version (KJV) of the Bible, which identifies the artists as wise hearted. The Modern English Version says, "You shall speak to all who are specially skilled, whom I have filled with the spirit of wisdom, that they may make Aaron's garments to consecrate him, that he may minister to Me as a priest"

(Exodus 28:3, MEV). And if you thought that the women had not been summoned as wise hearted, the Bible tells us that just as the men, they were called and identified as well. "And all the women that were wise hearted did spin with their hands, and brought that which they had spun, both of blue, and of purple, and of scarlet, and of fine linen. And all the women whose heart stirred them up in wisdom spun goats' hair" (Exodus 35:25–26, KJV). It is a beautiful thing that God has always counted with us!

It surprises me how many times the phrase "wise hearted" is repeated. This repetition indicates its importance. From Exodus 28 to Exodus 36, the phrase "wise hearted" is repeated seven times:

> And thou shalt speak unto all that are wise hearted, whom I have filled with the spirit of wisdom, that they may make Aaron's garments to consecrate him, that he may minister unto me in the priest's office. (Exodus 28:3, KJV)

> And I, behold, I have given with him Aholiab, the son of Ahisamach, of the tribe of Dan: and in the hearts of all that are wise hearted I have put wisdom, that they may make all that I have commanded thee; (Exodus 31:6, KJV)

> And every wise hearted among you shall come, and make all that the Lord hath commanded; (Exodus 35:10, KJV)

> And all the women that were wise hearted did spin with their hands, and brought that which they had spun, both of blue, and of purple, and of scarlet, and of fine linen. (Exodus 35:25, KJV)

> Then wrought Bezaleel and Aholiab, and every wise hearted man, in whom the Lord put wisdom and understanding to know how to work all manner of work for the service of the sanctuary, according to all that the Lord had commanded. (Exodus 36:1, KJV)

> And Moses called Bezaleel and Aholiab, and every wise hearted man, in whose heart the Lord had put wisdom, even every one whose heart stirred him up to come unto the work to do it: (Exodus 36:2, KJV)

And every wise hearted man among them that wrought the work of the tabernacle made ten curtains of fine twined linen, and blue, and purple, and scarlet: with cherubims of cunning work made he them. (Exodus 36:8, KJV)

This phrase "wise hearted" is translated in different versions of the Bible as "the skillful artists" or as "all who are skillful." In general terms, the "wise hearted" are spoken of as skillful workmen, both men and women of talent, experts with special abilities, people with great artistic capacity and with an artistic spirit filled with wisdom. And to the artists among the congregation of Israel, to those "wise hearted," God invited them to collaborate in the construction of the Tabernacle: "And every wise hearted among you shall come, and make all that the Lord hath commanded" (Exodus 35:10, KJV). Why does no one tell us that this is the way the Lord sees artists?

MOSES SPEAKS TO THE PEOPLE OF ISRAEL

It is interesting to note the biblical order and spiritual protocol that is established:

1. God speaks to Moses, who is the leader of the people, and showed him the work to be done.
2. God tells Moses who will do the work: Bezalel and Oholiab, with a team of wise-hearted people, a team of artists.
3. Moses speaks to the people. He summons "all the congregation of the children of Israel together" (Exodus 35:1) to communicate to them the things that the Lord commanded:

   - To keep the day of rest (Exodus 35:2–3)
   - The voluntary offering
   - The announcement of the construction of the Tabernacle (Exodus 35:10–29),
   - Telling the people that God called Bezalel and Oholiab and that He has equipped them for the work.

This is what Moses told the people: "See, the Lord has called by name Bezalel the son of Uri, the son of Hur, of the tribe of Judah...to design artistic works, to work in gold, in silver, and in bronze, and in the cutting of stones for settings and in the carving of wood in order to make every manner of artistic work" (Exodus 35:30, 32–33). Therefore, Moses concluded that Bezalel, Oholiab, and every man and woman wise at heart, emphasizing "in whom the Lord has put skill and understanding to know how to do all manner of work for the service of the sanctuary" (Exodus 36:1), would be the ones doing the work.

My attention is called to where it says, "And I have filled him with wisdom and understanding and in knowledge and in all manner of workmanship." What would happen to those filled with good intentions who were not equipped with the wisdom and knowledge to do the work? I understand that they would not participate in the project. They would be able to bring offerings: "Everyone whose heart stirred him and everyone whose spirit was willing came and brought the Lord's offering for the work of the tent of meeting and for all its service and for the holy garments" (Exodus 35:21). They needed to be equipped for this work, though.

Once the people of Israel were notified of the Lord's decision, Moses proceeded to call Bezalel and Oholiab and all men wise at heart to start the work. And again, we see the emphasis on those "in whom God had filled with wisdom," meaning men who possess the necessary skills for the work, but the text adds, "Moses called Bezaleel and Aholiab, and every wise hearted man, in whose heart the Lord had put wisdom, even every one whose heart stirred him up to come unto the work to do it" (Exodus 36:2, KJV). In other words, he called all the people who purposed in their hearts to work. Maybe some people had the skills but not the initiative, the desire to participate, or the determination to do the work; they were not called. Moses called unto all who were artistically equipped by God and whose heart was willing to come and work. It was an excellent combination: a talented team with a heartfelt desire to do the work.

NOTES

[1]https://www.maryloucaskey.com/what-does-it-mean-when-god-calls-you-by-your-name.html.

[2]James Strong, LL.D., S.T.D., *The New Strong's Expanded Exhaustive Concordance of the Bible*, (Nashville: Thomas Nelson, 2010), 108.

[3]Diccionario de La Lengua Esapañola©2005 Espasa-Calpe http://www.wordreference.com/definicion/ protocolo

[4]James Strong, LL.D., S.T.D., *The New Strong's Expanded Exhaustive Concordance of the Bible*, (Nashville: Thomas Nelson, 2010), 97.

[5]_____, *The New Strong's Expanded Exhaustive Concordance of the Bible*, (Nashville: Thomas Nelson, 2010), 43.

[6]_____, *The New Strong's Expanded Exhaustive Concordance of the Bible*, (Nashville: Thomas Nelson, 2010), 9.

[7]James Strong, LL.D., S.T.D., *The New Strong's Expanded Exhaustive Concordance of the Bible*, (Nashville: Thomas Nelson, 2010), 82.

[8]Robert Young, Young's Analitical Concordance to the Bible, (Peabody, MA: Hendrickson Publishers, 2011), 504.

[9]Jewish Encyclopedia. NY, 1910. http://jewishencyclopedia.com/articles/3918-caleb

[10]Flavio Josefo, Antiquities of the Jews, Book III, Chapter 6. https://www.sacred-texts.com/jud/josephus/ ant-3.htm

[11]James Strong, LL.D., S.T.D., *The New Strong's Expanded Exhaustive Concordance of the Bible*, (Nashville: Thomas Nelson, 2010), 109.

[12]James Strong, LL.D., S.T.D., *The New Strong's Expanded Exhaustive Concordance of the Bible,* (Nashville: Thomas Nelson, 2010), 107.

[13]http://torah-art.net/index.php/portrait-artist-marty-shoub.

[14]http://torah-art.net/index.php/Bezalel-son-light-2.

[15]James Strong, LL.D., S.T.D., *The New Strong's Expanded Exhaustive Concordance of the Bible,* (Nashville: Thomas Nelson, 2010), 7.

[16]————, *The New Strong's Expanded Exhaustive Concordance of the Bible,* (Nashville: Thomas Nelson, 2010), 11.

CHAPTER 4

TRANSCENDENCE
Bezalel's Legacy

> "Then the temple of God was opened in heaven,
> and the ark of His covenant was seen in His temple."
> (Revelation 11:19a)

FIGURE AND SHADOW OF HEAVENLY THINGS

I imagine, and here I am using my poetic license, that in the same way that King David jumped and danced while bringing the ark back to Jerusalem, Bezalel would not only have jumped and danced, but probably would have been so astonished that would have had no idea what to do or say. And in the end, he would have knelt down at the feet of the Heavenly Father in adoration at the sight of the Ark of the Covenant in the temple of God. The Bible tells us, in Revelation 11:19a, "Then the temple of God was opened in heaven, and the ark of His covenant was seen in His temple."

We studied in previous chapters about Bezalel's call and his training in the spiritual realm. We explored the extension of the work to be done, how the work was carried out, and how this work was done according to the model that had been shown to Moses. We have also seen how Moses reviewed the work before presenting it to God for approval and how the glory of the Lord filled the Tabernacle.

When I received Bezalel's revelation, I didn't know anyone who knew his story. And for decades, that was the norm. However, suddenly I saw how his story had begun to be known and, especially, how we artists were beginning to be inspired by his example. Definitely, he was an artist worthy of imitating, especially for his obedience to the divine mandate. But I understand that Bezalel did not work in isolation from the congregation. There was a whole support team, beginning with Moses and ending with the other artists, whom the Bible calls wise hearted. And I wonder, what has been the consequence or long-term result of the team's obedience. They were involved in the construction of the Tabernacle, its furniture, its accessories, and the clothing of the priests. And I wonder: Why was radical obedience essential? Why was submission to Moses necessary? How would all the symbolism of the Tabernacle have been altered if Bezalel had decided to change the design? What would have happened if Bezalel had wanted to make the Holy of Holies wider and more accessible to all priests? Or if he'd wanted to change the colors used in it, the materials, or the position of the furniture? What would have happened if Bezalel had said that the altar of sacrifice should not be placed in the courts because the blood of the sacrifices could frighten people or damage the design of the inner courtyard of the Tabernacle?

Something that stands out from Bezalel's behavior is his submission to Moses and his obedience to the instructions and specifications given. At no time do we read about his ego. On the other hand, we saw how Lucifer rebelled because he wanted to sit on the throne of God (Isaiah 14:13). Bezalel did not change the instructions, as Adam and Eve did, and we already know, sadly, what happened to them (Genesis 2:16). And although he had a whole team of artists working with him, he did not do as Korah did with Dathan, Abiram, and On when they organized 250 congregation leaders against Moses and Aaron (Numbers 16). And

I'm sure there were times when someone said something inappropriate or made a mistake.

I do not see Bezalel or his team in rebellion against Moses or in dispute with each other. And although the Holy Scriptures testify that the people called were highly skilled, the major mandate was to do the work according to the model that had been shown to Moses. There was no room for egos or for "I am the boss." I am sure that, although slaves, Bezalel and the other artists and collaborators of the Tabernacle had seen the artistic wealth of Egypt. And as slaves, they had participated in the construction of Pithom and Raamses as storage cities for the Pharaoh.

That is, they probably brought knowledge about construction and artistic work. However, they didn't compare some instructions with others. And if they thought about it, they didn't say it, because it doesn't appear written down or in the oral tradition. On the contrary, they submitted to the instructions of Moses given by God, though they might have made no sense to them. And when we say this, we say it thinking that when we receive an inspiration from God to do something, it might seem absurd or meaningless. This is often because maybe it's the first time it's been done and God, with His superior mind, is taking us along a path never traveled. And that is where we sometimes think that the knowledge we have is superior, and if we allow the ego to exalt itself, then we will discover that the divine plan was of much more excellence.

An example of this is Noah and the ark. Building a gigantic wooden ark when it had never rained was completely illogical. I'm sure many made fun of it. God gave him the design, measures, and purpose of the ark, and Noah obeyed: "Noah did this; he did all that God commanded him" (Genesis 6:22). As a result, after the flood, God blessed Noah (Genesis 9:1). There is a blessing as a result of obedience: "Moses looked over all the work, and indeed they had done it; as the Lord had commanded, so they had done. Then Moses blessed them" (Exodus 39:43), And the obedience and submission of Bezalel also made it possible for God's plan to not be corrupted or its purpose to be distorted. It seems to me that Noah and Bezalel, Oholiab, and the wise hearted were beyond their time and reflect what, centuries later, the apostle Luke would say: "So you also, when you have done everything commanded you, say, 'We are unprofitable servants. We have done our duty'" (Luke 17:10).

It is important to remember that we see things from a limited position, or as Paul says in 1 Corinthians 13:12, "For now we see as through a glass, dimly, but then, face to face. Now I know in part, but then I shall know, even as I also am known." God sees beyond what we see. He has no limits. And what, perhaps, is important for us at this time, in two or three years, it will no longer have the same meaning. But the things of God are eternal; they don't change. And there we find the wisdom of Bezalel and his team of wise hearted. They were radical in their decision to obey the command and did not lean on their own wisdom or think that what they understood would look prettier or be more practical or convenient for everyone. Instead, they did as Proverbs 3:5 says, "Trust in the Lord with all your heart, and lean not on your own understanding." This radical obedience to God's command has allowed us to have the message of the Tabernacle, as the first sanctuary, reach us today with the same force of approximately 3,500 years ago. And even more, the message of the Tabernacle as "figure and shadow of Jesus" has not weakened but has become increasingly powerful.

ABOUT THE TABERNACLE

It is interesting to note that God dedicated two chapters to the theme of the creation of the world; however, 50 chapters have been dedicated to the theme of the Tabernacle:

Exodus	13 chapters
Numbers	13 chapters
Leviticus	18 chapters
Deuteronomy	2 chapters
Hebrews	4 chapters and other references[1]

This emphasis on the message of the Tabernacle indicates that it is relevant, that it is valuable. There is something about it worthy of scrutinizing. We understand that when there is repetition in the Holy Scriptures, it is because the Holy Spirit is signaling that we should pay attention to the matter. Let us remember the call of Moses: "When the Lord saw that he turned aside to see, God called to him from out of the midst of the bush and said, 'Moses, Moses.' And he said, 'Here am I'" (Exodus 3:4). Or the call of the prophet Samuel: "The Lord came and stood, and He called as at other times, 'Samuel, Samuel.'

Then Samuel said, 'Speak, for Your servant listens'" (1 Samuel 3:10). Or when Jesus spoke to Martha: "He said: Martha, Martha, troubled and troubled you are with many things" (Luke 10:41). When Jesus says, "Truly, truly I say to you," through the book of the apostle John, each time, he points to a fundamental truth: "Jesus answered him, 'Truly, truly I say to you, unless a man is born again, he cannot see the kingdom of God'" (John 3:3). And here there are not two, but 50 chapters telling us about the Tabernacle.

Although we cannot explore in this chapter all the symbolism that the Tabernacle contains, we will point out some basic patterns to inspire and motivate contemporary artists so that when God shows his designs, the artistic ego does not interfere with God's design.

WHAT DOES THE TABERNACLE WANT TO TELL US?

I. Gordon, in his study *Jesus in the Tabernacle*, points out that in it, we find the image and typology of Jesus, the presence and holiness of God, the plan of salvation, and, finally, the dispensations and times of the plan of God.[2]

The story of the Tabernacle did not end in chapter 40 of Exodus. Nor did it end with the death of Moses or the conquest of the promised land, nor with the temple of Solomon. The rituals established with the law of Moses and carried out in the Tabernacle of the testimony have transcended generations and have come to our days with a primary purpose: to point us to Jesus as the mediator of a new covenant (Hebrews 8 and 9). A look at Hebrews 8:5a, and we find that the writer presents the Tabernacle as "shadow of the heavenly one." That is why God emphasized to Moses that he had to do it "according to the pattern shown you on the mountain" (Hebrews 8:5b). All of this, the writer emphasizes, is a symbol; that is, an equivalent or representation of the truth for the present time. However, everything changes with Jesus. Now Jesus is our High Priest (Hebrews 9:11). And in Hebrews 9:24–26, it continues to be emphasized that the Tabernacle was a copy of the true one and the sacrifices offered in it pointed towards the true sacrifice:

> For Christ did not enter holy places made with hands, which are patterned after the true one, but into heaven itself, now to appear in the presence of God for us. Nor did He enter to offer Himself often, as the high priest enters the Most Holy Place every year with blood that is not his own. For then He would have had to suffer repeatedly since the world was created, but now He has appeared once at the end of the ages to put away sin by sacrificing Himself.

How beautiful it is to see that the work you have done transcends centuries and serves to illuminate new generations. God asked Moses to raise a Tabernacle for Him to dwell among His people. That Tabernacle became the plan for redemption in three dimensions. And each structure, piece of furniture, color, material, and ritual indicate and typify the redemptive work that Jesus would do centuries later.

From the beginning of man's fall, God had a plan of salvation for the people. In Genesis 3:15, we see the curse of the serpent, but according to the law of double reference, it is also understood as the *Protoevangelium* (the first Gospel). God promised that through the seed or descendant of a woman would come one who would crush the head of Satan. This is considered the first promise of a Savior and the first great act of God's grace after man's rebellion:

> I will put enmity
>   between you and the woman,
>   and between your offspring and her offspring;
>   he will bruise your head,

and you will bruise his heel.

However, as I said before, with the Tabernacle, we see a whole prototype of what the redemption plan is in three dimensions and full color.

BEZALEL AND OHOLIAB FIGURE AND SHADOW OF JESUS

Bezalel and Oholiab typify Jesus. In other words, these two artists symbolize several of the characteristics that identify Jesus.

JESUS IS THE ALPHA AND THE OMEGA

Bezalel, like Jesus, was from the tribe of Judah: "It is well known that he [Jesus] was born a member of the tribe of Judah" (Hebrew 7:14).

The tribe of Judah was the first to march each time the camp moved from one place to another: "All who were numbered throughout the armies in the camp of Judah... They will march out first" (Numbers 2:9). It was the largest tribe. Oholiab, on the other hand, belonged to the tribe of Dan, and they were the last in the marching position: "All they who were numbered in the camp... They will set out in the back with their standards" (Numbers 2:31).

Jesus tells us, "I am the Alpha and the Omega, the Beginning and the End" (Revelation 1:8), and, "I am the First and the Last" (Revelation 1:17).

JESUS IS THE KING OF KINGS

Judah means praise (Genesis 29:35). Judah was one of the twelve sons of Jacob. Before Jacob died, he gathered his children and blessed them. To Judah, he said that his descendants would be the tribe from which kings would come: "Judah, your brothers shall praise you...your father's sons will bow down before you" (Genesis 49:8).

"The scepter shall not depart from Judah, nor a lawgiver from between his feet,until Shiloh comes; and to him will be the obedience of the people" (Genesis 49:10). For example, King David was from the tribe of Judah. Jesus is our "KING OF KINGS AND LORD OF LORDS" (Revelation 19:16).

JESUS THE RIGHTEOUS JUDGE

Dan means "He judged" (Genesis 30:6). Jesus is our just judge: "The Father judges no one, but has committed all judgment to the Son" (John 5:22).

JESUS AND HIS CHURCH

We have seen how Bezalel, along with Oholiab and his wise-hearted team, did all the things that the Lord had commanded Moses, and this included the Ark of the Testimony with its cover or mercy seat. We know about the ark from the moment Moses receives the instructions to do the Tabernacle (Exodus 25:9a). Immediately after he receives the instructions, the ark and the mercy seat are described (Exodus 25:10–21). Not only did the Lord order the ark, but he gave the exact description of how it should be done, what would be placed inside it, where it would be placed, and its purpose. We are allowed to know what the behavior of Aaron, the high priest, should be concerning the ark: "so that he will not die, for I [God] will appear in the cloud on the mercy seat" (Leviticus 16:2). This confirms what God said to Moses, that He would dwell in the sanctuary and, even more, "I will meet with you there, and I will meet with you from above the mercy seat, from between the two cherubim which are upon the ark of the testimony. I will speak with you all that I will command you for the children of Israel" (Exodus 25:22).

We are told that the families of the sons of Kohath would be in charge of the ark (Numbers 3:29–31) and how they should prepare the ark for the move: "And when the camp sets out, Aaron will come, and his sons, and they will take down the covering curtain, and cover the ark of the testimony with it"(Numbers 4:5). And something that seems extremely beautiful to me is that the work was so well done that nothing stopped the presence of the Lord from it. The Bible tells us, "Moses went into the tent of meeting to speak with Him, and he heard the voice of One speaking to him from the mercy seat that was on the ark of the testimony, from between the two cherubim, and He spoke to him" (Numbers 7:89). The ark symbolizes the throne of God and his presence. It is the most sacred furniture in the sanctuary; therefore, the Tabernacle was really created to house the ark. And the ark represents the presence of God dwelling among the people.

We are told in Exodus 37:1 that Bezalel made the ark. This implies that he directly made it or was the main artist in the process. He was an anonymous hero, because, once the construction was finished, we only find Bezalel's name during the time of King Solomon. Once Solomon was declared king, he decided to go to Gibeon because the meeting tabernacle was there. And we are told that King David had brought the ark, "And the bronze altar that Bezalel the son of Uri, the son of Hur, had made was set before the tabernacle of the Lord. And Solomon and the assembly sought it out *to seek the* Lord" (2 Chronicles 1:5). After this, we do not hear more about Bezalel; however, his legacy had an interesting journey, especially the ark.

Although after the construction of Tabernacle is over, we do not know what happened to Bezalel, but his work, like that of Oholiab and the other artists, continued to reap the fruit. For example, on the mercy seat with its two cherubim, the presence or Shekinah of God continued to manifest. Shekinah is a Hebrew word meaning "residence." And because God was present in this cloud, a person in sin could not stand before the mercy seat; even the high priest could die.

REBELLION OF THE PEOPLE

Once the Tabernacle was finished, the people began their march to the promised land. And the Bible tells us, "And it was, when the ark set out, that Moses said, 'Rise up, O Lord, and let Your enemies be scattered, and let them that hate You flee before You'" (Numbers 10:35). However, along the way, the people rebelled. Ten of the twelve spies sent by Moses to the promised land brought a negative report. As a consequence, the people talked about stoning Moses and Aaron. They were saved from this fate because the glory of the Lord was shown in the Tabernacle (Numbers 14:10). As punishment for the rebellion, God told them that only Joshua, Caleb, and the young would enter the promised land. The people then changed their minds and decided to go, but they did not take the ark (Numbers 14:44). As a result, the inhabitants of the mountain on which the Israelites went up defeated them, and many died. Because of their disobedience, they had to stay for 38 years in the desert, until all that generation died. Only Joshua, Caleb, and those who were children and young when the people left Egypt survived.

Interestingly, there is a moment in which Moses says that he made the ark:

"Then the Lord said to me, 'Cut two stone tablets like the first ones and make a wooden Box to put them in. Come up to me on the mountain, and I will write on those tablets what I wrote on the tablets that you broke, and then you are to put them in the Box.'

"So I made a Box of acacia wood and cut two stone tablets like the first ones and took them up the mountain. Then the Lord wrote on those tablets the same words that he had written the first time, the Ten Commandments that he gave you when he spoke from the fire on the day you were gathered at the mountain.

The Lord gave me the tablets, and I turned and went down the mountain. Then, just as the Lord had commanded, I put them in the Box that I had made—and they have been there ever since." (Deuteronomy 10:1–5)

Some interpret this moment as one of jealousy or envy on the part of Moses; however, in Exodus 32:16, we read that the first two tablets were the work of God. Moses broke them, and as a consequence, he was told by God to come upon the mountain again and God would write them again. According to Dake, "this confirms the fact that the ark remained in the camp, and that when

Moses came down with the tablets of stone he put them in the ark." This is the same ark mentioned in Exodus 25:10–22. Also, in Deuteronomy 31:9, 24–26, we are told that Moses wrote the law and instructed the Levites to put it in the Ark of the Covenant without mentioning again that he put it in the ark he had made. It seems to me that when he says, "in the ark which I had made," he means that he received the order and, under his direction as the leader of the congregation, it was built. In addition to this, the Bible testifies to the character of Moses when Mary and Aaron, both brothers of Moses, speak against Moses because of his wife: "Now the man Moses was very humble, more than all the men on the face of the earth" (Numbers 12:3).

A NEW BEGINNING
Some Highlights Of The Ark's Trajectory Until It Disappears

Once Moses died, Joshua was the leader. And the ark, carried on the shoulders of the priests, would guide them to cross the Jordan on their way to the promised land: "When you see the ark of the covenant of the Lord your God and the Levite priests carrying it, then you shall set out from where you are and go behind it"(Joshua 3:3)." Upon arriving at the Jordan, the priests carrying the ark set foot in the waters of the river, the waters opened, and the people could pass without getting wet. Once the people passed by, the priests carrying the ark left the Jordan, and the waters returned to their level.

THE DESTRUCTION OF JERICHO

The ark played a prominent role in the destruction of Jericho. Once in front of Jericho, the Lord spoke to Joshua, and among His instructions, he said, "Take up the ark of the covenant. Seven priests bearing seven ram's horn trumpets shall be in front of the ark of the Lord" (Joshua 6:6). And they would do it for seven days. And on the last day, before the cry of victory of the people, the walls fell (Joshua 6:20).

THE TRIBE OF BENJAMIN

The tribe of Benjamin sinned by raping the concubine of a Levite (Judges 19:25), and the other tribes decided to fight against them as punishment. However, despite being stronger than the tribe of Benjamin, they lost both battles against them. After the last battle, they decided to go to the Ark of the Covenant: "The children of Israel asked the Lord (because the ark of the covenant of God was there in those days... The Lord said, 'Go up, for tomorrow I will give them into your hands'" (Judges 20:27–28). God gave them the strategy, and they defeated the tribe of Benjamin.

THE CAPTURE OF THE ARK

When the people confronted the Philistines, they were defeated. It is then that the people asked that the ark accompany them. They understood that the presence of God was manifested where the ark was:

> When the people came into the camp, the elders of Israel said, "Why has the Lord struck us today before the Philistines? Let us bring the ark of the covenant of the Lord out of Shiloh to us, that it might come among us and rescue us out of the hand of our enemies."

> So the people sent to Shiloh, that they might bring from there the ark of the covenant of the Lord of Hosts, who dwells above the cherubim. And the two sons of Eli, Hophni and Phinehas, were there with the ark of the covenant of God.

> When the ark of the covenant of the Lord came into the camp, all Israel shouted with a great shout, so that the ground was in an uproar. When the Philistines heard the sound of the shout, they said, "What does this great shout in the camp of the Hebrews mean?" Then they understood that the ark of the Lord had come into the camp. (1 Samuel 4:3–6).

However, "Now the ark of God was taken, and the two sons of Eli, Hophni and Phinehas, died" (1 Samuel 4:11). This was an event they did not expect. When the messenger arrived, Eli, the high priest, immediately asked for the ark:

> The messenger answered and said, "Israel has fled before the Philistines, and there also has been a great slaughter among the people. Your two sons also, Hophni and Phinehas, are dead. And the ark of God is taken."
> When he mentioned the ark of God, Eli fell from off the seat backward by the side of the gate. And his neck broke and he died, for he was an old and heavy man. And he had judged Israel forty years.
>
> His daughter-in-law, Phinehas' wife, was pregnant, about to give birth. And when she heard the news that the ark of God was taken, and that her father-in-law and her husband were dead, she kneeled down and gave birth, for her pains came upon her…
>
> She named the child Ichabod, saying, "The glory is departed from Israel," because the ark of God was taken, and because of her father-in-law and her husband. She said, "The glory is departed from Israel, for the ark of God is taken." (1 Samuel 4:17–19; 21–22)

For the first time, the ark was in the hands of the enemy, but the Philistines had no idea what awaited them. They did not know that they were dealing with a living God and not with images. Therefore, they decided to put the ark in the house of Dagon, god of vegetation:

> When the Philistines took the ark of God, they brought it into the house of Dagon and set it by Dagon. When the Ashdodites arose early in the morning, Dagon had fallen upon his face to the ground before the ark of the Lord. And they took Dagon and set him in his place again. When they arose early on the next morning, again Dagon was fallen

upon his face to the ground before the ark of the Lord, and the head of Dagon and both the palms of his hands were cut off upon the threshold. Only the *torso* of Dagon was left to him. (1 Samuel 5:2–4)

The ark was a curse for the Philistines. The statue broke, but worse, tumors broke out on the Philistines, and the earth was filled with mice:

> When they saw what was happening, they said, "The God of Israel is punishing us and our god Dagon. We can't let the Covenant Box stay here any longer." So they sent messengers and called together all five of the Philistine kings and asked them, "What shall we do with the Covenant Box of the God of Israel?"

> "Take it over to Gath," they answered; so they took it to Gath, another Philistine city. (1 Samuel 5:7–8)

> So they sent the Covenant Box to Ekron, another Philistine city; but when it arrived there, the people cried out, "They have brought the Covenant Box of the God of Israel here, in order to kill us all!" So again they sent for all the Philistine kings and said, "Send the Covenant Box of Israel back to its own place, so that it won't kill us and our families." There was panic throughout the city because God was punishing them so severely. (1 Samuel 5:10–11)

Seven months after his capture, the ark was returned to Bet-semes, in Israel (1 Samuel 6:12). From Bet-semes, the ark was sent to Quiriat-jearim, where it stayed twenty years (1 Samuel 7:1–2).

DAVID TRIES TO TAKE THE ARK TO JERUSALEM

When David was king over all Israel, he made Jerusalem his capital. King David tried to bring the ark to Jerusalem, but the instructions established in the law of Moses were not followed, and they put the ark in a new car instead of carrying it on the shoulders of the priests. And "When they came to the threshing floor of Nakon, Uzzah reached out and took hold of the ark of God, because the oxen had stumbled. The Lord became angry against Uzzah, and God struck him down on the spot for his irreverence. He died there beside the ark of God" (2 Samuel 6:6–7). Because of this, the ark was taken to the house of Obed-Edom: "The ark of the Lord remained at the house of Obed-Edom the Gittite for three months, and the Lord blessed Obed-Edom and his entire household" (2 Samuel 6:11).

However, the opposite of what happened to the Philistines happened in Obed-Edom's house; God blessed him. David then decided again to bring the ark to Jerusalem; for this, he prepared a place to build the Tabernacle and concluded that the instructions given in the law of Moses must be followed: "Then David said, 'No one may carry the ark of God except the Levites since the Lord chose them to carry the ark of the Lord and to minister before Him always'" (1 Chronicles 15:2). And the Bible says, "The sons of the Levites lifted up the ark of God just as Moses commanded, with the poles on their shoulders, according to the word of the Lord" (1 Chronicles 15:15). The ark returned to Jerusalem with joy, sacrifices, music, and dance:

So David, the elders of Israel, and the leaders of the thousands went to bring up the ark of the covenant of the Lord from the house of Obed-Edom with rejoicing. Since God helped the Levites who carried the ark of the covenant of the Lord, they sacrificed seven bulls and seven rams. Now David was clothed in a fine linen robe, *as were* the Levites who carried the ark, the singers, and Kenaniah, the conductor of singing and singers. David *himself* wore a linen ephod. So all Israel brought up the ark of the covenant of the Lord with a shout and with the sound of the ram's horn and with trumpets and cymbals, making music on harps and lyres. Now as the ark of the covenant of the Lord was entering the City of David, Michal the daughter of Saul was looking down from the window, and when she saw King David dancing and spinning, she despised him in her heart. (1 Chronicles 15:25–29).

Once King David died, Solomon occupied the throne of David, his father. And one of the first things he did was go to Gibeon because there was the tabernacle, (2 Chronicles 1:3). And in

Gibeon, there was also the bronze altar that Bezalel had made (2 Chronicles 1:5), but the ark had been brought from Quiriat-jearim to Jerusalem.

And as I said before, it is with King Solomon that the name of Bezalel and his genealogy is mentioned again. But it is only mentioned. There are no ceremonies or recognition for having made such significant and lasting pieces 680 years before. Once Solomon completed the construction of the temple, he decided to bring the ark to the temple: "The priests and Levites brought up the ark of the Lord, the tabernacle of the congregation, and all the holy implements that were in the tabernacle" (1 Kings 8:4).

However, the Bible tells us that when the veil was discovered, there was the ark: "Then the temple of God was opened in heaven, and the ark of His covenant was seen in His temple. And there came lightning, noises, thundering, an earthquake, and great hail" (Revelation 11:19).

The ark was an instrument to house the presence of God. As we have seen, from the middle of the cherubs, the presence of God was manifested, and He spoke to the high priest. The ark was, therefore, a symbol of the Lord 's presence, guidance, protection, and testimony of a living God for pagan peoples and, above all, joy among the people of Israel. For us today, the ark typifies Jesus: His human nature and His divine nature.

Therefore, Bezalel was not only an artist, but through his work, he was project director and a teacher, in this way fulfilling God's calling in his life. Fifty chapters are dedicated to the story of the Tabernacle, and Bezalel and his team are the main characters. Also, their obedience and submission allowed the powerful message of the Tabernacle to come all the way to today. And to think that God used a wonderful group of artists to accomplish a significant divine project: the first sanctuary where the Lord would dwell among His people. What an amazing privilege!

Once the Tabernacle was completed, we don't know what happened to Bezalel and his team, but the Tabernacle, and especially the ark, reflected how gifted and dedicated to the truth of God this team was. My prayer is that it is your ART that speaks for you.

NOTES

[1] C.W. Slemming, *Made According to Pattern*. (Fort Washington, PA: CLC Publications, 1999), 13.

[2] I. Gordon, *Jesús en el Tabernáculo*. n.d.

CONCLUSION

TOWARDS A
THEOLOGY OF ART

The story of Bezalel still amazes me: an artist called by God. Even more, I still remember the moment when I discovered his story. After discovering Bezalel, I dreamed of God calling my name and setting me apart to be an artist. I dreamed of using art as an instrument of transformation for God's glory. I also continue to have an immense desire to see that in the same manner that God shows the design of the Tabernacle to Moses, He will do the same to us. And since then, I proposed in my heart to tell the story of Bezalel to every artist. This book is an extension of that dream. I wanted for you to discover Bezalel and especially that you, too, appropriate the six gifts that God gave Bezalel, Oholiab, and the group of wise-hearted artists who collaborated with Bezalel.

After I discovered Bezalel, I continued to conduct research into his artistic calling, the work of the Tabernacle, and his accomplishment. In the beginning, the information was limited, but I was hungry for God and for the arts. During the process, I had dreams and visions about God's plan for the arts. That kept me going. And I discovered a divine pattern. I called it the theology of art. Why did I call it this? I have a very simple answer. Theology comes from two Greek words: "Theos," which means God, and "logy," which comes from "logos" (word); therefore, theology is the study of God as He is revealed in the Bible, the Word of God. So, when I say theology of art, I am studying what God says in the Bible about art. I think the story of the calling of Bezalel includes the foundation or guidelines of a possible theology of art.

Bezalel is also a wonderful role model for contemporary artists. Probably, there were moments when Bezalel felt the desire to add his personal or particular touch to the Tabernacle. Nevertheless, the Bible says that Bezalel made everything "as the Lord commanded Moses." Bezalel made Moses look good before the Lord. And these are major words. The commandment that Moses received was unique. Remember that the Lord had convocated a reunion in the mountain that lasted forty days and forty nights. There, He gave the Ten Commandments to Moses, the general laws that would serve as a guideline to a nation that was barely forming, and He showed how the Tabernacle would be made. Bezalel's obedience made Moses look good before God. I can say Moses stood with his head held high before the Lord and, with great satisfaction, that all was made "as it was shown on the mountain."

The Tabernacle, in our day, is a testimony of the plan of salvation for our lives, a shadow of what was to come, JESUS. And the obedience of Bezalel made the Lord's message arrive intact. I understand that Bezalel is to us artists an example of obedience, submission, and character contrary to what happened, for instance, with Korah. We have seen how Bezalel successfully completed the task to which he was called and capacitated.

When I wanted to learn about art in the Bible, I asked God, and He directed my steps to Exodus 31 and 35, and there I met Bezalel, his calling, and his accomplishment. Through these passages, I found the biblical foundation of what I understand can be the theology of art.

Therefore, I envision a theology of art:

- That proclaims that art is God's will and a gift from the God Creator to humanity.
- That declares that artists are creators by divine nature and that in the moment of our creation, God

breathes His Spirit, giving us His breath of life, imparting in us His Creator Spirit.

- That understands artists are chosen and called by name by the Lord.
- That announces that God fills artists with His Holy Spirit.
- That celebrates that God empowers artists with the spirit of wisdom.
- That states that God invests artists with the spirit of understanding.
- That pronounces that God has endowed artists with the spirit of knowledge.
- That rejoices that God has enabled artists with the spirit of art and creativity.
- That delights that God has inspired artists with the ability to teach.
- That makes known that God loves for artists to obey and submit to God and leaders.
- That acknowledges that artists are under the shadow and special protection of the Most-High God.
- That understands that artists are a shadow born from the light of the Creator.
- That knows that artists are the reflection of the Creator God, small creators.
- That encourages artists to recognize God and His Word as their light.
- That teaches artists that their lives must be completely dedicated to God.
- That recognizes that artists are worshipers, that we belong to the tribe of Judah (praise), called to emphasize the glory of God.
- That teaches artists to reflect the greatness of our God.

- That knows that only the artist who loves God and respects His laws can fulfill the commitment to create art for the glory of God.

- That recognizes that artistic talent is not limited to the Church alone. God has given it to us for the blessing of humanity, for "glory and honor" of his name. And if we only glorify God in the Church, how will we enlighten the secular world that does not know Him? In the same way that rulers and peoples saw God through the work developed by Joseph, Solomon, and Daniel, humanity can see and glorify God through our artistic work.

I understand that as artists called by God, we need to shine and reflect His glory. And it is in this moment when, as artists, Jesus is telling us, "You are the light of the world. A city that is set on a hill cannot be hidden. Neither do men light a candle and put it under a basket, but on a candlestick. And it gives light to all who are in the house. Let your light so shine before men that they may see your good works and glorify your Father who is in heaven" (Mathew 5:14–16).

APPENDICES

APPENDIX A
The Work to Complete

According to the order of appearance in the Bible, from Exodus 25 to Exodus 30, God commands Moses to do the following:

THE ARK OF THE COVENANT

Exodus 25:10–22

Measurements

- Length 3.67 feet (1.12 meters)
- Width 2.23 feet (68 centimeters)
- Height 2.23 feet (68 centimeters)

Specifications:

- The ark will be made of acacia wood.
- It will be covered inside and out with pure gold.
- It shall have a gold border round it.
- It will have gold rings in the four corners. Two rings shall be in the one side of it, and two rings in the other side of it, for a total of four rings of pure gold.
- It will have poles of acacia wood overlaid with gold.
- The poles will be put into the rings by the sides of the ark so that the ark may be borne with them, and they will be kept on the rings of the ark all the time.

Purpose:

- "You shall put into the ark the testimony which I shall give you." (Exodus 25:16). Hebrews 9:4 says, "which contained the golden censer and the ark of the covenant overlaid with gold, containing the golden pot holding the mana, Aaron's rod that budded, and the tablets of the covenant." (The tables of the covenant are the Ten Commandments, Deuteronomy 10:1–5).

MERCY SEAT

Measurements:

- Length 3.67 feet (1.12 meters)
- Width 2.23 feet (68 centimeters)
- It is the mercy seat (the top of the ark), made of pure gold.
- The mercy seat, along with the two cherubim at its extremities, will be made from one single piece of material.
- The mercy seat will go on top of the Ark of the Covenant in the Most Holy (Exodus 26:34).

Purpose:

- "I will meet with you there, and I will meet with you from above the mercy seat, from between the two cherubim which are upon the ark of the testimony. I will speak with you all that I will command you for the children of Israel" (Exodus 25:22).

THE CHERUBIM

Specifications:

- Made from gold wrought by a hammer.
- One cherub at one end, and the other cherub at the other end. The cover and the cherubim at both extremes will be made from one single piece of material.
- The wings of the two cherubs will extend upwards in such a manner that they will cover the top of the ark, and they will be one in front of the other. The faces of the cherubim will look towards the mercy seat.

FURNITURE AND ACCESSORIES

The Table for the Showbread (Bread of the Proposition)

Exodus 25:23–30

Measurements:

- Length 3 feet (90 centimeters).
- Width 1.5 feet (45 centimeters).
- Height 2.23 feet (68 centimeters).

Specifications:

- Table made from acacia wood overlaid with pure gold.
- It will have a gold border around it.
- It will have four rings of gold, which will be at the four corners.
- Over against the border, shall the rings be for the staves to bear the table.
- Two rods of acacia wood, overlaid with gold, that the table may be carried with them.
- The dishes, spoons, pitchers, and bowls with which to pour drink offerings will be of pure gold.
- The table will be outside of the veil, at the north side (Exodus 26:35).

Purpose:

- "You shall set the showbread on the table before Me always" (Exodus 25:30).

The Gold Lampstand (Candlestick of Gold)

Exodus 25:31–39

Measurements:

- The lampstand, with all its utensils, will be made of 75 pounds (34 kilos) of pure gold. Some researchers calculate the weight was around 107 pounds since the exact weight of a gold talent is unknown.

Specifications:

- The lampstand, its foot or base, and cane will be wrought by hammer.
- From its sides will come six branches, three branches from one side of the candlestick and three from the other side of the candlestick.

- There will be three cups in the form of almond flowers in one arm, with an apple and a flower, and three cups in the form of almond flowers in the other arm, with an apple and a flower.
- In the cane of the candlestick shall be four bowls made like unto almond flowers, with their knops or apples and their flowers.
- There shall be an apple under the first two branches of it, and an apple under the next two branches of it, and an apple under the last two branches of it, according to the six branches that proceed out of the candlestick.
- Its apple and its branches shall be of one single piece of material.
- All shall be one beaten work of pure gold.
- Seven lamps, the tongs thereof, and the snuff dishes shall be of pure gold.
- The candlestick will be in front of the table at the side of the Tabernacle to the south (Exodus 26:35).

Purpose:

- "You shall make its seven lamps, and they shall light its lamp so that they may give light to the area in front of it" (Exodus 25:37).

THE TABERNACLE

The Curtains of Twined Linen

Exodus 26:1–6

Measurements:

- The length of each curtain will be 42 feet (12.6 meters).
- The width of each curtain will be six feet (1.8 meters).
- All the curtains will have the same measurements.

Specifications:

- The tabernacle will have 10 curtains of twined linen of blue (a mixture of indigo and dark red), purple, and scarlet, with cherubim of cunning work.

- Five of the curtains will be coupled one with the other. Also, the other five curtains will be coupled one with the other.
- Bows in blue fabric on the edge of one of the curtains of the extreme of the first selvage in the coupling; and likewise, in the uttermost edge of another curtain, in the coupling of the second.
- 50 bows in one curtain and 50 bows in the edge of the curtain that is in the coupling of the second, that the loops may take hold one of another.
- 50 taches of gold and couple the curtains together with the taches so it will be one unit.

The Curtains of Goat Hair

Exodus 26:7–13

Measurements:

- Eleven curtains of the same measurements.
- The length of each curtain will be 45 feet (13.5 meters).
- The width of each curtain will be 6 feet (1.8 meters).

Specifications:

- The curtains of goat's hair to be a covering upon the tabernacle.
- Five curtains coupled by themselves, and six curtains by themselves.
- The sixth curtain will be doubled in the forefront of the tabernacle.
- Fifty bows on the edge of one curtain that is outmost in the coupling, and 50 bows in the edge of the curtain which coupleth the second.
- Fifty taches of brass. The taches will be put into the bows to couple the tent together that it may be one.
- The remnant that remains of the curtains of the tent, the half curtain that remains, shall hang over the backside of the tabernacle.
  - On one side, 1.5 feet (45 centimeters).
  - On the other side, 1.5 feet (45 centimeters) of what remains of the length of the tent curtains.
  - It shall hang over the sides of the tabernacle on one side and on the other to cover it.

Purpose: Cover for the Tabernacle's roof.

A Cover of Rams' Skins

Exodus 26:14a

Specifications:

- Rams' skins dyed red.

Purpose:

- To weatherproof the tent.

A Cover of Porpoise Skins

Exodus 26:14b

Specifications:

- Cover for the tent.

Purpose:

- To weatherproof the tent.

THE TABERNACLE STRUCTURE

Exodus 26:15–37

The Vertical Boards

Exodus 26:15–25

Measurements:

- Length of each board: 15 feet (4.5 meters)
- Width of each board: 2 feet (68 meters)

Specifications:

- The vertical boards for the tabernacle will be of acacia wood and will be put vertically.
- Each board will have two tenons to unite with each other.
- 20 boards to the south side.
- 40 sockets of silver under the 20 boards: two sockets under one board for its two tenons and two sockets under another board for its two tenons.

- For the second side of the tabernacle, on the north side, 20 boards and its 40 sockets of silver: two sockets under one board, and two sockets under another board.
- For the sides of the tabernacle, westward, six boards. Two boards for the corners of the tabernacle in the posterior part.
- They will be double underneath, coupled together above the head of it unto one ring.
- This will be for both of them: they will form the two corners. There will be 16 boards with silver sockets: two sockets under one board, and two sockets for the other.

Bars of Acacia Wood

Exodus 26:26–30

Specifications:

- Five bars of acacia for the boards of one side of the tabernacle.
- Five bars for the boards of the other side of the tabernacle, and five bars for the boards of the side of the tabernacle, for the two sides westward.
- The middle bar in the center of the boards will go from one end to another.
- The boards will be overlaid with gold, and the rings will be of gold where the bars will be placed. The bars will be overlaid with gold.
  Note: The vital function of the boards was to strengthen the structure of the Tabernacle by uniting the boards and maintaining them firmly together.

Purpose:

- "And thou shalt rear up the tabernacle according to the fashion thereof which was shewed thee in the mount" (Exodus 26:30).

The Veil

Exodus 26:31–33

Specifications:

- Veil of blue fabric, and purple, and scarlet, and fine twined linen. It will be made with cherubs of cunning work.

- It will hang upon four pillars of acacia wood overlaid with gold.
- Their hooks shall be of gold, upon four sockets of silver.
- The veil will hang under the taches, and behind the veil will be the Ark of the Testimony.
- The veil, 30 feet from the Tabernacle's aperture.

Purpose:

- The veil shall divide the holy place and the most holy.

Tabernacle's Door

Exodus 26:36–37

Specifications:

- Of blue, purple, and scarlet fabric, and fine twined linen, wrought with needlework.
- Five pillars of acacia wood for the curtain overlaid with gold.
- The hooks will be of gold, too.
- Five sockets will be cast of brass for them.

Purpose:

- A curtain for the tent's entrance.

THE ATRIUM AND THE DOOR

Exodus 27:9–19
   The Atrium

   Exodus 27:9–19

Measurements and Specifications:

- To the south side will be curtains of twined linen for the atrium, of 150 feet (45 meters) of length for one side.
- Its pillars will be 20, with its 20 sockets of brass.
- The hooks of the pillars and moldings will be of silver.
- Likewise, for the north side, there shall be curtains of (150 feet) 45 meters in length and its 20 pillars and 20 sockets of brass.

- The hooks of the pillars and their fillets will be of silver.
- And for the width of the court/atrium on the west side shall be curtains of 75 feet (22.5 meters) with its ten pillars and ten sockets.
- And the width of the court/atrium on the east side will 75 feet.
- The curtains of one side of the gate shall be 22.5 feet (6.75 meters) with three pillars and three sockets.
- For the other side, there will be curtains of 22.5 feet (6.75 meters) with three pillars and three sockets.
- The door of the court/atrium, there will be a curtain of 30 feet (9 meters) of blue fabric, purple, and scarlet, and fine twined linen, wrought with needlework: and their pillars shall be four, and their sockets four.
- All the pillars round about the court shall have silver moldings; their hooks shall be of silver, and their sockets of brass.
- The length of the court/atrium will be 150 feet (45 meters), the width 75 feet (22.5 meters) by each side, and height of 7.5 feet (2.25 meters); its curtain of fine twined linen, and their sockets of brass.
- All the vessels of the tabernacle in all the service, all the pins, and all the pins of the court/atrium shall be of brass.

Atrium's Door

Exodus 27:16

Specifications:

- For the atrium's door, there will be a curtain of 30 feet (9 meters).
- Blue fabric, purple, and scarlet, and fine twined linen, of needlework.
- Four pillars with its four sockets.

The Bronze Altar

Exodus 27:1–8

Specifications:

- Altar of acacia wood.
- 7.5 feet of length (2.25 meters).

- 7.5 feet of width (2.25 meters), the altar will be square.
- 4.5 feet of height (1.35 meters).
- Horns in its four corners.
- The horns shall be of the same piece of the altar, overlaid with brass.
- Make pans to receive the ashes, shovels, basins, meat hooks, and firepans.
- All the vessels will be made of bronze.
- Grill of brass made as a net; and upon the net, four bronze rings in the four corners, under the altar's border, so the net reaches up to the middle of the altar.
- Bars for the altar, bars of acacia, overlaid in bronze.
- The bars shall be put into the rings so they will be on the two sides of the altar when it's transported.
- Hollow with boards, as it was shown on the mountain.

SACRED WARDROBE

Exodus 28:1–4

Specifications:

- Materials: gold, blue fabric, purple, scarlet, and fine linen.
- Holy wardrobe for Aaron.
- Wardrobe: a vest, ephod, mantle, tunic stitched in squares, a tiara, and a belt.

Purpose:

- For glory and beauty.
- To consecrate Aaron and his sons as priests.

Ephod of Gold

Exodus 28:6–7

Specifications:

- Of blue fabric, purple, and scarlet, and fine twined linen, with cunning work.
- It will have two shoulder pieces that will be joined at the two edges so they can be joined together.

- Two onyx stones, with the names of the 12 sons of Israel engraved in them.
- Six of the names in one stone and six other names on the other stone, all in order by birthday.
- Two chains of pure gold, in the form of braided laces, fastened to the ouches.

The Belt

Specifications:

- Cunning needlework, over the ephod.
- Material: gold, blue fabric, purple, scarlet and of fine twined linen.

The Vest

Exodus 28:15–21

Specifications:

- Of cunning work
- Similar to the ephod materials: gold, blue fabric, purple, and scarlet, and fine twined linen.
- Square and double, 9 inches (25 cm)
- It will have four lines of stones
    - The first line will consist of a sardius, a topaz, and a carbuncle (emerald).
    - The second row shall be an emerald, a sapphire, and a diamond.
    - The third row a ligure, an agate, and an amethyst.
    - The fourth row a beryl, an onyx, and a jasper.
    - They shall be set in gold in their inclosings.
    - There will be 12 stones, as the names of the sons of Israel.
    - Like the engravings of a signet, everyone with his name shall they be according to the 12 tribes.

The Mantle of the Ephod

Exodus 28:31–35

Specifications:

- The mantle of the ephod was all in blue fabric.

- There will be an opening in the middle of its superior part.
- It shall have a binding of woven work around the opening, as it were the hole of a habergeon, that it be not rent.
- Beneath upon the hem of it, it will have pomegranates of blue, and of purple, and of scarlet, round about the hem; and bells of gold between them round about: a golden bell and a pomegranate, another golden bell and another pomegranate upon the hem of the robe round about.

Purpose:

- It shall be upon Aaron to minister.
- Its sound shall be heard when he goes into the holy place before the Lord, and when he comes out, so he does not die.

Plate of Pure Gold

Exodus 28:36–38

Specifications:

- Plate of pure gold.
- Engraved, like the engravings of a signet, HOLINESS TO THE LORD.
- It will be put on a blue lace that it may be upon the tiara; in the front.

Purpose:

- The plate will always be in front of Aaron so he obtains grace before Jehovah.

TUNICS, MITER, BELTS, TIARAS, AND UNDERPANTS

Exodus 28:39–43

Specifications:

- Embroidered coat/tunic of fine linen.
- A mitre or tiara of fine linen.
- A girdle/belt of needlework.
- Coats/tunics, girdle/belt, and bonnets or tiaras for Aaron's sons.
- Linen underwear from the loins to the thighs.

ALTAR TO BURN THE INCENSE, PILE OF BRASS, ANOINTING OIL, AND THE INCENSE

Altar to burn the incense

Exodus 30:1–10

Measurements:

- Square: 18 square inches (45 cm)
- 3 feet (90 cm) of height

Specifications:

- Made from acacia wood.
- The horns shall be of the same piece.
- Overlaid with pure gold: the top, the sides, and the horns.
- It will have a crown of gold round about.
- Two golden rings under the crown of it, by the two corners, upon the two sides, and they shall be to place the bars and be transported.
- Bars of acacia wood and overlaid with gold.
- Altar position: in front of the veil that is by the ark of the testimony, before the mercy seat that is over the testimony.

Purpose:

- Aaron shall burn sweet incense every morning upon it when he prepares the lamps.

Metal Fountain

Exodus 30:17–21

Specifications:

- Metal base (brass).
- Placed between the tabernacle of the congregation and the altar, with water in it.

Purpose:

- To wash. With it, Aaron and his sons shall wash their hands and their feet upon entering the tent of the testimony so they do not die.

- Also, when they come near to the altar to minister, to burn offerings made by fire unto the LORD: they will wash their hands and their feet so they do not die.
- It shall be a statute forever to them.

The Oil of Anointing

Exodus 30:22–33

Specifications:

Take from the finest spices:

- Pure Myrrh, 18 pounds
    - Sweet cinnamon, half, 9 pounds
    - Sweet calamus, 9 pounds
    - Sweet cassia, 18 pounds
    - Olive oil, 1.5 gallons
- Mix

Purpose:

- It will be oil for the holy anointing
- To anoint:
    - The tent of reunion
    - The Ark of the Pact
    - The table and all its utensils
    - The candlestick and all its utensils
    - The altar of incense
    - The altar of holocaust and all its utensils
    - The pile and its base
    - Aaron and his sons

The Incense

Exodus 30:34–38

Specifications:

- Sweet spices, stacte, onycha (tree resin), galbanum (originally, it was obtained from a plant that produces a milky substance of rubbery consistency), and clean incense (aromatic resin and rubbery), each one of the same weight or quantity (ratio/equal parts).
- With it, a perfume will be made (incense), a confection after the art of the apothecary, tempered together, pure, and holy.

- Some of it shall be beaten very finely. A part of it will be put before the testimony in the tabernacle of testimony/congregation.
- This incense won't be made in the same proportions for proper or personal use because this proportion is specific, consecrated to Jehovah.

Purpose:

- The incense will be holy for Jehovah. Whosoever makes an incense like this to use it as perfume will be cut off from his people.

APPENDIX B
ART IN THE PROPHETIC PLAN OF GOD

Months after learning about the calling of Bezaleel and after accepting God's invitation in my own life, I had a vision. I saw two gear wheels, two golden wheels. Each wheel was the same as the other one. In my spirit, I asked what the meaning of what I was seeing was, and a voice within my spirit started to explain that one wheel represented the people that God was calling and separating for the events of the end times. "Every thread represents a person," the voice said. And I saw in my spirit how a huge hand would pull people from different places and put them together to build the wheel. He emphasized that every thread had to be identical to the others: "No one was more important than the other." Then He said, "The second wheel represents my Word, and when the two wheels engage together, they will roll along perfectly."

The reason why each thread has to be the same size, the voice explained to me, is that when the wheels engage together, each thread should fit exactly into the space of the other wheel, like a puzzle, so that when they engage, they can roll softly and within each other. "If one thread is larger than the other, the wheels will not be able to engage together. Thus, they will not move," He said. In my vision, when the two wheels engaged and started to roll, streams of water came out from the union. "The water," the voice of my spirit continuously said to me, "is the Holy Spirit covering the earth." And the instrument that God was using so that this could happen was art; I saw the water falling upon Puerto Rico and down unto Central and South America and the rest of the world.

Then I heard the voice again speaking to my spirit and telling me that the time would come when we would see different places and even countries closed to the preaching of the Word in all traditional ways, but that there would be artists from different parts of the world who were prepared by God and capable of spreading the message of salvation through art. And I understand that like Esther, we have been called for this time.

APPENDIX C
LIZETTE AYALA LETTER (1980)

June 19th, 1980

Bretton Hall College of the Arts
West Bretton, "New Wakefield"
West Yorkshire, England

Alma,

[…] Look, Rafael invited Mayra and me to talk about our experiences in Christian theater at a youth assembly. I was going to tell him no at first, but the truth is I have never had the experience to testify on that particular subject or to support him, not only biblically but as a way to create conscience and impact the non-believer. When I was preparing to talk about theater, I wanted to bring Bible verses that sustained my position. And do you know what, Alma? You should remember something you told me once and I never forgot. I am referring to the Bible verse of Exodus 31 that narrates God's calling to two men, Bezaleel and Aholiab, and how God told them through Moses and before the children of Israel that He had filled them of:

1. Spirit of God
2. Wisdom
3. Intelligence
4. Science
5. In **all art**

This order has a significant logic because, at first, there is a difference between science and art. Science **knows**, and art **creates**. To create (art) requires knowledge (science). To know you need wisdom. And wisdom comes from God, who gives it abundantly and without reproach (James 1:5). I used this verse that you taught me a long time ago, and even though I didn't remember where it was, I found it. I also learned with a Biblical Dictionary that Paul preached at the Ephesus theater (Acts). I talked about my experiences, and to end, he told them that **drama seasoned the Word**. He also said that theater was very **effective** because of its audiovisual platform. This means the person retains 50% of what it sees and 10% of what it hears. Therefore, theater guarantees that the person will retain 60%, and the Lord will take care of the other 40%. This indicates that for a non-believer, it is more effective than simple preaching, where he would only retain 10% of what he heard. Clarifying, of course, that he wasn't against it because the teaching was biblical, but proving the effectiveness **of theater**.

Mayra used all that she learned in your classes given in Guaynabo for dramatization at churches. This is so you know that your words weren't gone with the wind; they were treasured, and today, we shared them with other churches.

Lizy

NOTE:

Lizette is no longer with us but this letter that she sent me when I was a student in Bretton Hall College of the Arts, England, is one of my most precious treasures.

APPENDIX D
OPENING NEW PATHWAYS

Both Lizette Ayala's letter and this recognition are witnesses of a long journey. And although, in its beginnings, it seemed that the Word fell into a vacuum, today I realize that what Isaiah 55:11 tells us has been fulfilled:

> So shall My word be that goes forth from My mouth;
> it shall not return to Me void,
> but it shall accomplish that which I please,
> and it shall prosper in the thing for which I sent it.

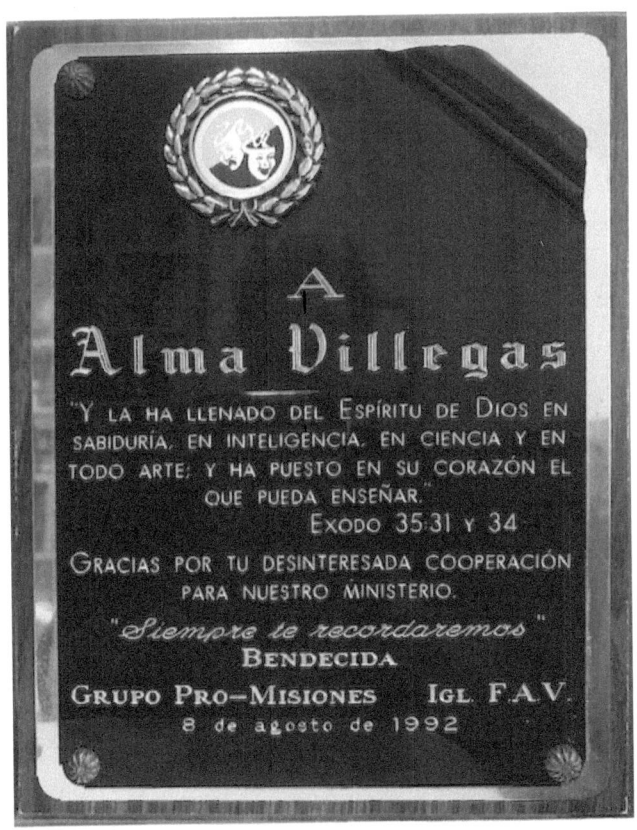

BIBLIOGRAPHY

Blue Letter Bible. *"Dictionary and Word Search."* Blue Letter Bible. 1996–2012.

Clarke, Adam. *Commentary on the Bible.* <http://www.sacred-texts.com/bib/cmt/clarke/exo.htm>.

Copeland, Kenneth. *The Kenneth Copeland Word of Faith Study Bible.* Modern English Version (MEV). Lake Mary, Florida: Published by Passio, 2017.

Dake, Finis Jennings. *Dake's Annotated Reference Bible.* Lawrence, Georgia: Dake Publishing, Inc., 2014.

Diccionario de la lengua española, © 2005 Espasa-Calpe, <http://www.wordreference.com/definicion/protocolo>.

Gordon, I., *Jesús en el Tabernáculo,* n.d.

Habershow, Ada R. *Outline Studies of the Tabernacle.* Grand Rapids, MI: Kregel Publications, 1974.

Hershberger, Ervin N. *Seeing Christ in the Tabernacle.* Harrisonburg, VA: Vision Publishers, 1995.

https://archive.org/details/ofplatobanquet00platrich/page/90/mode/2up.

https://biblestudentsdaily.com/2016/09/02/study-1-an-introduction-to-the-tabernacle-and-its-purpose/.

http://torah-art.net/index.php/portrait-artist-marty-shoub/.

https://www.biblegateway.com.

https://www.merriam-webster.com/dictionary.

Instituto Cultural Álef y Tau, A.C. *Biblia Peshitta en español.* Nashville: Broadmand & Holman Publishing Group, 2006.

Kalish, Edward Ephraim. *Bezalel, Son of Light*. Video.

Levi, David M. *The Tabernacle: Shadows of the Messiah*. Grand
Rapids, MI: Kregel Publications, 2003.

Lledó, Emilio. *El concepto "poiesis" en la filosofía griega*. Madrid:
Editorial DYKINSON, S.L., 2010.

Otto, Christ John. Bezalel, *Redeeming a Renegade Creation*. MA:
Belonging House Creative, 2015.

Rand, W. W. *Diccionario de la Santa Biblia*. San Jose: Editorial
Caribe, s.f.

Slemming, C. W. *Made According to Pattern*. Fort Washington, PA:
CLC Publications, 1999.

Strong LL., S.T.D., James. *The New Strong's Expanded Exhaustive
Concordance of the Bible*. Red Letter Edition. Nashville:
Thomas Nelson, 2010.

Young, Robert. *Young's Analytical Concordance to the Bible*.
Peabody, MA: Hendrickson Publishers, 2011

Vine, W.E. Edited by Merrill F. Unger, Th.M., Th.D., Ph.D. and
William White, Jr., Th.M., Ph.D. *Vine's Complete Expository
Dictionary of Old and New Testament Words*. Nashville:
Thomas Nelson, 1996.

ABOUT THE AUTHOR
Alma Villegas, PhD, ThD

Author, Poet, Theater Director/Playwright/Independent Producer, Theater in Education Specialist, and Theology of Art Researcher

A LOOK AT THE IMPACT OF THE ARTS IN MY LIFE

My career began as a physics, biology, and chemistry teacher. However, during my first years as a teacher, I realized that the students were missing something that would season their lives. New paths had to be opened for them, and that something that they lacked, that way to open, was the way of art. Thus, with a group of high school students, I began my adventures in theater and the discovery of the impact that art can have on people's lives.

With this transformative vision, I returned to the University of Puerto Rico (UPR) to study theater. After finishing my studies at the UPR, I left for England, where I studied at Bretton Hall College of the Arts. In Bretton Hall, in addition to studying medieval theater and Shakespeare, I was able to study with several of the precursors of theater in education, such as actor and director John Hodgson. Upon my return from England, I continued studying at New York University (NYU), in the Department of Music and Performing Arts Professions, where I obtained a PhD in Educational Theater. And in August 2014, I received a doctorate in Christian Theology from the International Miracle Institute (IMI), Pensacola, FL.

GOD FULFILLS HIS PURPOSE IN US

I accepted Jesus as my Savior at the age of 16, at which time I started to attend the youth meetings at the *Iglesia Defensores de la Fe*, located on Comerio Street in Bayamón, with Rev. Leonardo Castro as pastor and Rafael Torres Ortega, Esq., as the youth pastor. I became an active member of the youth society. Together with a wonderful group of young people, I was one of the founding members of Grupo de Avivamiento, a choir that visited and continues to visit practically every town on the island of Puerto Rico, different countries throughout Latin America, and some US states with the message "Tiempo para cambiar" (Time to Change). Along with the Grupo de Avivamiento, I was able to visit the Dominican Republic, New York, New Jersey, Connecticut, Venezuela, Colombia, Guatemala, Mexico, and Chile. I experienced thirteen years of spiritual growth and, at the same time, an intense evangelistic and missionary work.

As I grew in the Lord and developed my leadership within the youth, I also had the opportunity to attend the University of Puerto Rico (UPR) and obtain a Bachelor of Science with a major in agriculture and home economics. These studies prepared me for and allowed me to work at isolated and/or special communities to minimize their physical, economic, and socio-cultural isolation. This would allow me to take my first steps towards the realization of a dream that had just started to be awakened: to combine art with missionary work in places where there was a great spiritual, economic, and socio-cultural need. I also attended the University of Bridgeport, where I received a master's degree in education with a concentration in biology. After all of this, finally, I found the courage to go back to the University of Puerto Rico to study theater.

Throughout those formative years, I had the opportunity to preach, to be a Sunday school teacher, and to create for the local church the first Sunday school workshops for the children's teachers. However, it was in the area of art, more specifically in the area of theater, where my petition to God, "Lord make me a woman of ideas," started to be manifested within the Church as well as in the schools where I worked as a biology teacher. With the first ideas that I was developing and the incipient creative inspirations that I now understood were coming from God, I became, at a very early age, an independent theater producer and director, lighting, stage, and costume designer, actress, and playwright. In those early days, I had no choice: if I wanted to do theater, I had to do it myself. It was a great school.

Even though, at Luis Pales Matos High School in Santa Rosa, Bayamon, I was a physics teacher, I decided, with a group of students, to create a journalism workshop, starting the newspaper *Clarín*. This project, with the help of the school faculty, hosted the creation of the *Semana Palesiana* (Palesiano Week), responding to the students' lack of positive identity with the school. During that week, we painted murals, published a special newspaper issue commemorating the week, and filled the school with signs saying, "Estudiante Palesiano" (Palesiano Student). We also presented the Night of *Clarín*, a theater production that was written and directed by the student members of the journalism club; we invited well-known performing artists and civic and cultural leaders in Puerto Rico to come and give concerts and conferences to us. Among them, we had the presence of Jacobo Morales (actor, poet, and filmmaker) as a facilitator at a conference about Puerto Rican Culture and Sylvia del Villar (who offered an outstanding recital performance on the poetry of Luis Pales Matos). We hosted a literary contest and a program through WIPR Channel 6, a government-owned station, with Jesus Latimer, Dr. Margot Arce de Vazquez, and Ana Mercedes Pales (Luis Pales Matos's daughter). What impacted my life the most is that as of that first week of celebration, the theme "Estudiante Palesiano" (Palesiano Student) became part of the students' vocabulary, establishing a new episode in the life of the school that is still ongoing.

This experience exposed me to an unknown aspect of art, which, at the same time, brought a lot of questions. For the first time since my conversion, I was involved in secular work where art was the principal source, and the positive impact on the student body was highly visible. Would it be possible that God could use me as a positive-change instrument for something that many considered "worldly"? The answer was positive. And I witnessed how the arts were an agent of change in the student community.

Three years later, I became a teacher at Jardines de Caparra High School, another school in Bayamon. The small size of the school impacted me, as did the lack of artistic and cultural activities; there were practically none. It was then that I organized some theater workshops, and from them came the creation of Taller de Teatro Guariquén (Guariquén Theater Workshop). Guariquén is a Taino word meaning, "Look, come, and see." Tainos were the indigenous people of Puerto Rico. During the five years that I spent working with the theater group, I taught almost all aspects of theater arts, and I wrote, adapted, and developed around ten theater plays and screenplays for concerts that I was able to produce and direct.

This artistic work with the students was reflected throughout the community, which, in turn, started to experience the transforming power of art and its impact in society, bringing, as a consequence, to the members of the theater workshop all of their support. As an indirect result, many young people accepted Jesus as their personal Savior, and they were later followed by their parents. I emphasize "indirect result" because, as a teacher in the public education system, my goal was educational and cultural. And again, unexpected results were being manifested. What was moving those students to have an experience with God? I also witnessed how the arts were an agent of change, not only in the student community, but in the community at large. And here, I witnessed the second transformation, but this time, it went beyond the student community. This time, it reached the families of the students.

From the beginning of my development in the arts, I used theater, music, poetry, body movement, dance, pantomime, photography, biblical texts — especially the Psalms — as vehicles for education, personal development, and worship God. My artistic work, both carried out in the school and in the Church, was successfully presented throughout the island on television and in schools, hospitals, cultural centers, music conservatories, hotels, theaters, and churches. So, my pastor decided to give me a new challenge. By then, Rev. Rafael Torres Ortega was the senior pastor of the church. He allowed me to work next to him as an assistant producer of Encuentro (Encounter), an innovative Christian television program based on interviews with prominent Christian leaders and community leaders in general. My job was to design the introduction, select the music, and be the hostess for the guests before the beginning of the program, and sometimes I would be interviewed or become an interviewer if the guest didn't show up. This program was the basis for what later became one of the first Christian stations in Puerto Rico.

A CONVERSATION AND A CHALLENGE

One afternoon, as I was driving back home, God visited me in the car. I still remember the intensity of what I felt that day. The Lord spoke to my spirit about a calling. He told me that He was placing a different option before me than the one I had faced, that if I wanted to continue serving Him the same way, He would bless and prosper my way, but He was opening a new way before me. I understood in my spirit that the way would not be an easy one and that many years would pass by before I would see the manifestation of what God was speaking about. I had heard many times in church services through different preachings that God always has the best option. At that time, I started crying because I understood that my life was going to change dramatically, and I said, "Lord, I choose what you are offering me."

I always remember my last day at work on my way to study in England. As I was talking with one of the teachers, I looked at one of the blackboards, and God gave me a vision, and again I saw a long road, but since I was so committed and concentrated on my calling, I felt no fear nor intimidation about it. Besides, under the euphoria of the moment, I calculated that when the Lord spoke about many years, He was probably referring to five years. I am sure that the Lord smiled and felt at ease to know that I was not like the children of Issachar, experts in discerning the times. Maybe, if I had understood what God was speaking to me about, I would have remained in the comfort of my house and at the school where I was working. After all, I was serving the Lord and enjoying the positive results of my work.

Exodus 31 and 35, my conversations with God, the visions and prophetic words all confirmed the calling of God in my life; they reinforced my vocation towards theater, and they birthed the dream of continuing my advanced studies in theater and to study what the Bible said about art. I wanted to be ready for the arrival of the manifestation of my calling. I dreamed about teaching theater as the instrument of education, inspiration, healing, and transformation of communities around the world. I also dreamed of a supernatural manifestation of the spirit of creativity for the Church.

ART AS AN INSTRUMENT OF CHANGE

After the calling of God to my life, the doors to attend Bretton Hall College of the Arts in England and New York University in New York City opened widely. I left Puerto Rico to study and, at the same time, start a career in art that has brought me great satisfaction.

One of the most significant projects of my work in New York has been working in the prevention of HIV and the use of drugs within the Puerto Rican community. A program in creative arts was created and implemented to educate and empower the people who were affected by HIV/drugs throughout the community in general. Art was also used as an instrument of spiritual and emotional healing. As part of the strategy to work in the community, we opened a space called Manny Maldonado Theatre Gallery (1995–2005) to use it as a place of experimental and alternative theater. This was the first theater gallery that was opened in Williamsburg, Brooklyn, and it became a pioneering artistic movement of social transformation and of emotional and spiritual healing for a community that, until then, had been strongly whipped by drugs and HIV/AIDS.

As part of the work done at the theater gallery, we had 30 art exhibitions, 12 live theater performances, 10 outdoor festivals (concerts, theater, and dance), four indoor concerts, three spoken-word events, and a video festival. An art program was created for the community in general, including percussion and, on many occasions, piano, musical theory, dance, creative writing, and singing. We designed two public art exhibitions in two of the parks within the community, both dedicated to the AIDS epidemic; the United Nations documented one of them. A community that used to be identified primarily by its epidemic of drugs and AIDS, Williamsburg is today recognized in New York City and outside its limits as artistic and prosperous.

I understand that we were not the only ones in the transforming process of the community, but we played a leading role. Witnesses to this are the numerous awards, newspaper articles, radio interviews, and television programs that came to document the prevention work done through the arts, such as CNN in Spanish and Eyewitness News, ABC TV. Witnesses to this are also the presentations and demonstrations of the use of music in HIV prevention at national conferences, such as the Center for Disease Control and Prevention (CDC) in Atlanta, Georgia. And even more, participation in international conferences, such as the 12th World AIDS Conference in Geneva, Switzerland, and Women 2000: Women's Health Concerns in Latin America and the Caribbean in the 21st century, sponsored by the United Nations. And even an invitation to the White House, in Washington, D.C.

Thus, again, we witnessed another transformation. This time, the change was greater and more powerful because it reached an entire community and transformed drug addicts and people living with AIDS or HIV. God makes no distinction of person. He longs to reach all mankind.

In the area of theater production, the work done in the musical Civil War Voices by James R. Harris stands out. In it, I was part of the production team that won the Outstanding Production of a Musical Award at the 11th Midtown International Theater Festival (2010). The work won 11 nominations and six awards.

I was part of the Project CREO team, an Arts InterFACE initiative, which has developed an art project for children nationwide in Ecuador. During my stay in Quito, Ecuador, I gave seminars on acting, dramaturgy, and art theology. In addition, I directed an adaptation of the Song of Solomon, which I called *This is my Beloved*. It included body expression, music, and theater.

CONNECTING HEAVEN AND EARTH THROUGH THE ARTS

My mission in life is to make new paths and, in that journey along these new paths, transform people's lives and restore their creative spirit using the arts, especially the theater, as an instrument of inspiration, healing, and transformation.

I feel grateful to God because I understand that He gave me wisdom, knowledge, and, above all, the gift of art as an instrument to transform and literally save lives. The Bible tells us in Ephesians 3:20–21, "Now to Him who is able to do exceedingly abundantly beyond all that we ask or imagine, according to the power that works in us, to Him be the glory in the church and in Christ Jesus throughout all generations, forever and ever. Amen."

And I am a witness of such a creative abundance of God.

FOR INFORMATION ABOUT...

Theater Workshops and Theology of Art Seminars

www. TheGiftofArtInfo.com
www. AlmaVillegas.net

almavillegas@aol. com

Books

Bezalel Series

Bezalel, an Artist Called by God
Bezalel, an Artist Called by God: Study Guide and Creative & Artistic Activation

For those who prefer reading short books, I divided *Bezalel, an Artist Called by God* by its three main themes. It is also a good alternative for the young artist in your life.

God Chose an Artist: Bezalel's Call
Artist? God Has Six Gifts for You
Obedience and Submission, The Key to Bezalel's Success

Prophetic Performance Series

DECREES: Prophetic Performance
SIMBOLIC ACTIONS: Prophetic Performance
PROPHESIES, VISIONS & DREAMS: Prophetic Performance

Creative and Artistic Activation

The Creative Power of the Word of God for the Artist

Amazon.com

www.ingramcontent.com/pod-product-compliance
Lightning Source LLC
Chambersburg PA
CBHW030939240526
45463CB00015B/583